LOVE LOST, Love Regained

JEAN MARIE CAMPBELL

Love Lost, Love Regained: Overcoming an Unhappy Childhood

Personal correspondence and questions regarding speaking engagements are welcomed and will be forwarded to the author unopened.

All scriptural references are quoted from The New American Standard Bible, copyright, 1972, by The Lockman Foundation.

With the exception of the author herself, all names of characters have been changed as well as some minor events and their sequences.

Library of Congress Cataloging in Publication Data

Campbell, Jean Marie.
Love lost, love regained.

1. Campbell, Jean Marie. 2. Christian biography—United States. 3. Adolescent girls—United States—Psychology. I. Title.
BR1725.C23A35 1983 280'.4 [B] 83-10423
ISBN 0-310-43491-2

Edited by Julie Ackerman Link
Designed by Martha Bentley

Printed in the United States of America

83 84 85 86 87 88 / 10 9 8 7 6 5 4 3 2 1

With great affection this book is dedicated to

God
my Father

Janice A. Stuckey
His ambassador of love to my world

and to
Hundreds of My Students
whose similar backgrounds
prompted this retelling

CONTENTS

PREFACE

WORTHLESS. ANXIOUS. HOPELESS. What a narrow range of feelings for any child to bear in the early stages of development; and yet in the days of my youth, these emotions became my steady companions. Created largely by real life situations *and my subjective interpretation of them,* fear and confusion became a painful way of existence reaching far beyond those early formative years. Their poisonous roots would contaminate and limit how I perceived myself, my relationships with others, and my notions of God for years to come.

Recently scores of books have been written to give adults an understanding of the turmoils in their own lives, and that is good. This book, however, presents an entirely different side of the issue: what happens to the hurting, ignored, or abused child who is victim of adult problems? What of the titanic scars that may have been transmitted by one's very own mother or father? By unloving parents who remain together? By alcoholic parents? By parents who divorce? By abusive parents? How does one overcome the haunting voices from the past? The phantom pains of rejection and condemnation? Is victory even possible?

One of the most sobering verses of the Bible on the issue of personal development is found in Proverbs. "Train up a child in the way he should go, even when he is old he will not depart from it." Much like the house built upon rock, the child who experiences love and security will have greater fortitude to face the future with confidence. But what of those whose foundations lack the solid healthy structure of warmth and acceptance? The tragic truth in the verse suggests that the destructive experiences of childhood as well as the constructive ones affect behavior throughout the adult's lifetime.

To some degree all of us still shadowbox with undying images from the past. Some of us are merely pulled to our yesterdays by imaginary strings, while others are jerked and bound by invisible steel chains. The heavy, restraining links that do not break easily. Fetters that have not been waved away by the magic wand of time, awareness, or religious experience. It is to these latter individuals that I address *Love Lost, Love Regained.*

You will find no pat answers here. Instead I shall simply tell portions of my story as honestly as I dare without bringing unnecessary embarrassment to the family members who have sometimes helped me and sometimes hurt me. I beg their forgiveness, and yours, if I have grossly misrepresented the encounters that have shaped my twenty-some years of life. It is now impossible for me to go back and learn if or when and where my vision was obstructed along the way. Keep in mind that the story is fundamentally my own story—no one else's—told through my eyes as only I could see it. Because of this, I've focused more on the battlefield of my private civil war rather than on giving rigorous detail to outward events.

What is the bottom line in sharing my pilgrimage with you? I want to offer road signs along the Journey of Hopeful Struggles that may be ahead for you, too. I want to say that God's love has made all the difference in my world, though total wholeness is something I may never experience in this lifetime. I want to explain that we who steadily seek inner healing can perhaps know God best because we not only come to him for renewal, but cling to him for *survival.* And lastly, I want to proclaim that *some of the sweetest lilies can be found in the valley,* despite our resistance to being there.

Amid the countless complexities and variables in my life and in yours, please know that we can face our futures with hope. My concluding prayer is that the Father will be glorified in this retelling. My desire is that you may be enlightened, encouraged, and strengthened in your own pursuit of a fuller life because I have been vulnerable enough to tell you about mine.

1 Chronicles 29:11
Summer, 1983

ACKNOWLEDGMENTS

My sincerest gratefulness to these contributors in my life:

To *Catherine Marshall* for providing excellence in Christian literature my whole lifetime and for her personal words of encouragement as I prepared this book.

To *Ralph Milton Small* who believed in me so strongly that he opened the first major door to a writing career.

To those friends at *The Zondervan Corporation* for graciously investing their confidence and enthusiasm in my story and for adopting this young author into their writers' circle. I am indebted forever.

To my two mentors, *Joseph F. Roher* and *Roger K. Barrett.*

To the memory of *Joanna Louise Wood* and to others at my church and college who've continued to express love and interest in my career and in my life.

I love you all,
Jean Marie

PART I

LOVE LOST

". . . yet He will by no means leave the guilty unpunished, visiting the iniquities of fathers on the children and on the grandchildren to the third and fourth generations."

Exodus 34:7

Tempest Child

Yes
quite early in life
you learn the storm
never dies.
In it you kneel
a naked prisoner
fiery cold
against the desolate bitter winds
that whip your youthful flesh
to bared raw wounds.
In it you kneel
a weeping captive
among wet waves of despair
that thunder the barren wilderness
of your lonely, weary road.
You kneel and you pray
and you pray
for the violent showers to cease.
And you wonder who
or what
can stop the stinging rain
that pours from your own young eyes.
Yes
quite early in life
you learn the storm
within
never dies.

1

Twelve

I YAWNED WIDE and tapped my copy of *The Scarlet Letter* against the shiny glass wall. Four, maybe five goldfish at my corner of the tank darted impulsively at the intrusion of sound, and a zebra trio flitted playfully through faded algae strands; but the little red jewel fish did not move. I tried again for its attention. This time the small crimson form arched and jerked inches leftward until it buoyed to the surface once more on its side. It was sick and close to dying. I could tell.

"Campbell, Jean?"

I continued my stare at the tiny vermilion body. Why did it have to die? Why? Why this one and not the others? It was speckled so pretty, pretty red. *So* pretty.

"Jeanie?" came the interruption from across the waiting room. The woman in white smiled and swung open the hallway door for me to enter. "You're next."

I nodded, fumbled for my purse, and stood. Before I reached the nurse, I turned to glance at the aquarium one last time. "I think it's a jewel fish in there," I told her and pointed. "A red one. It's sick. Probably should take it out so it doesn't infect the others. Maybe it'll get well if it's by itself." I paused then added, "Do you think?"

"I don't know," the middle-aged woman replied, "but thanks for telling me. I'll be sure to look into it later. You raise fish?"

"Naw," I said and brushed by her into the narrow corridor, "no fish."

She motioned to the right and cupped her hand sideways. "Examining room C is available."

I followed close by and continued, "No fish at home, but I got a cat. A big black one I named Popcorn. And Bernie—that's my one brother—he's got a dog. It's really a mutt and it pants all over you. Always panting! I don't like dogs," I said matter-of-factly, "just cats. But I'd take an aquarium any day if I was allowed. Fish look so peaceful, don't you think? Even that little red one out there. It's struggling just to live. Do you think fish can feel? Do you think that one knows it's sick? And close to dying? Do you?"

"My, my, my!" she chuckled. "You certainly are full of questions today." The nurse hesitated a moment at the doorway to the examining room, then turned to look at me. "I suppose fish can feel. I think so. Why not?"

"Yeah," I returned, "why not? But, but I hate to see that jewel fish suffer. What I mean is I hate—"

She drew up her hand like a policeman at an intersection. "You sure are worried about that little red fish out there. Don't fret, Jeanie, we'll take care of it. Now, why don't you go on in so we can get your weight and temperature taken before Dr. Bradford's ready? Cheer up, okay? And just set your things on the yellow table over there."

"No more fish talk, honest," I answered. I entered the small room and hastily tossed my purse and paperback book on the desk top. I don't know why I wasn't more careful. The book stayed in place, but the small purse flew off the side and onto the floor. "Practically light as a feather," I said nervously and kneeled down to pick up its scattered contents. "Nothing in it but a comb and a pocket notebook and a couple papers from school today."

She took a step backward and squinted her large brown eyes. "Don't forget your pen. It rolled under the examining table. Way back there."

Fully on the floor now, I groped with one twisted arm under the couch. "I'm sorry, ma'am. I didn't mean for it to fall. *It just fell.* It . . . it was an accident and I feel bad because—"

"Just relax, Jeanie. It's fine. No harm done. Just take your time."

"Yeah, but I don't like to . . . to . . . oh, nothing. I got it now," I whispered and crawled back out. Awkwardly I stuffed the pen into my purse, brushed my pants, and clutched at the table leg to pull myself up faster. When I swung around from my half-kneel position to a full stand, my right foot slipped behind me and caught on a movable metal tripod that held a special intensity light. I hadn't seen or felt it until it was too late.

"Got it!" the nurse cried out as she caught the center pole on its way down. "Whew! We should order bigger examining rooms next time, right?"

She tried to make a little joke of the whole incident, but I was visibly startled. It scared me, and I hurt my knee badly when I slammed it down against the hard floor. How it throbbed! My face flushed hot red to keep from crying and I stuttered, "It's me. I'm sorry. I'm really sorry. Nothing I do is right anymore. Wherever I go . . ."

"Come on, Jeanie," she said and pulled me up. "Everything's okay, isn't it? It was just an accident. Can you believe one time I knocked over this very same light? I did. About eight months ago. Only no one was behind me to catch it." She smiled warmly and continued, "So you're a pretty lucky young girl."

"No. No, you don't understand," I quivered. "It's me. It was my fault. And I get careless and I'm just clumsy. I . . . I don't mean to be but sometimes I am."

"Everything's all right," she said. "Why don't you have a seat and relax? Maybe read your book until the doctor is ready? What is it you brought with you anyway?"

My knee still ached and I leaned down to massage it. I took a deep breath. "It's one I picked up at the school bookstore last week. *The Scarlet Letter*. I'm almost done with it."

"Good grief! What grade are you in?"

"Seventh."

"And how old are you?"

"Twelve," I replied.

She reached for the book on the desk. "I didn't get through this one until I was at least a senior in high school or first year in college. I can't even remember it's been so long." She glanced at the binder then thumbed casually through the pages. "Nathaniel Hawthorne, huh? That's pretty steep for a youngster your age, do you know that?"

"I . . . I like to read a lot," I said and quietly slid into the chair. I was feeling more comfortable now. More at ease. Fortified in my world of reading. "Books keep me busy and out of trouble. And I really like that one."

"You understand this?" she asked with a touch of amazement in her voice.

"Some parts are hard, but I think so. I think I understand. This woman's name is Hester and she has a little baby but she won't tell who the father is. See, her husband's back over in England," I mentioned, lifting my index finger for emphasis, "and she's over here.

Those people—Puritans they were—are out to make her pay. So they get her to wear the letter *A* all the time because it stands for . . . for . . . you know . . . adultery."

"That's the book, all right. Well, whiz kid, more power to you!"

"Whiz kid?" I repeated. "Did you like it when you read it?"

"Let's put it this way: I was more into science and chemistry, definitely not literature, back then."

"Oh," I stated. "I gotcha now."

She only laughed.

"I think when I'm done I want to go back through it again." I stopped to think. "It has a lot in there. You know, especially how people think and feel deep inside."

The nurse raised her eyebrows and nodded her head in agreement. After she put the book down on the table beside me, she had a new burst of enthusiasm. "Say—do you think I could get you to stand on the scales five or ten seconds now? And while I take your temperature you can get back to your book and Lady Hester? How's that sound?"

"Sure," I said. "I'm ready if you are."

By the time Dr. Bradford came through the door I had studied and memorized all the items on his utensil cart: one large glass jar of tongue depressors (big and small), three thermometers in a metal tube container, some multicolored vials and ampules of this and that, a box of gauze, assorted wrapped bandages, three kinds of scissors, forceps, a great big bottle of alcohol marked POISON in brilliant red letters, five syringe packages (but no needles), some swabs, two rolls of white cloth tape, and a blood pressure kit. That was just the top shelf.

"So how are we doing today, Miss Jeanie?" Dr. Bradford asked and smacked my leg hard. He was a jolly, round man who always greeted me the same way.

I shrugged my shoulders. "Well, if you really want the truth—"

"That's the only way to tell it!" he noted cheerfully.

"I don't exactly feel so hot. My mother was kind of worried and set up the appointment for today after school. She should be here in a little bit to pick me up. At least I hope so."

He flipped open the brownish folder that bore my name. "Why don't you tell me how you feel?"

"It's my stomach. It's still my stomach."

"Let's see," he said and fingered through some stapled papers in the file folder. "I gave you a prescription last month, the fifteenth. Didn't that help?"

"Kind of. But it always seems tense." I directed my hand over the area. "Right here. And sometimes I throw up when it gets real upset."

Dr. Bradford scratched his head and responded. "Do you think it's what you're eating or could you be gobbling your food down too fast? Something like that?"

"Don't think so. Sometimes I *can't* eat. Sometimes I just pick at the food."

"Does it hurt, oh, let's say half an hour or so after you've had a meal?"

"No, not especially. I mean I don't notice it more then than at other times in the day."

"Hop up here and lie down," he said, tapping his palm on the examining table.

When I followed his instructions he pulled my sweater back several inches. He moved his fingers on my abdomen at one place then another. It tickled at first. "This hurt now? Right here where I press?"

"No. No, it's a different kind of pain I'm talking about. I don't know how to describe it."

Dr. Bradford wheeled around for my folder, opened it, and grabbed at his white pocket for the silver ballpoint pen. "Can you be very specific and tell me how it feels when it hurts? Try."

"Most of the time it's kind of a slow ache," I said, "if you know what I mean. And then it can get like it's all twisted up. Real, real tight inside. I even wake up sometimes with that feeling in the middle of the night."

He scribbled a few notations on my chart then told me to sit up. For the first moment or two he listened intently to my heartbeat. "It's a little fast today, but nothing to worry about. How about your throat? Open up."

The dry wooden tongue depressor in the very back of my mouth made me gag a little. And, of all times, I sucked in air around his hand for a huge, huge yawn.

"It's somewhat red back there. You getting enough sleep?"

"I'm in bed enough, if that's what you mean. But I don't know how much sleep I get. In hours, I mean. Sometimes I can sleep and sometimes I can't. I try to. I want to. But sometimes I can't."

"Swing around here, Jeanie. Let's talk."

Dropping my legs over the side of the cushion made enough room for him to sit beside me on the examining table. Dr. Bradford patted his hand on my knee again as he thought of the right words to administer, perhaps, an inner healing.

"Jeanie, Jeanie," he said real low, almost in a whisper. "I've known your family for years and years, and you ever since you were this big." He pulled his hands apart, leaving only inches between them to describe my once-infant size.

"Why, I was beside your mother's hospital bed when her heart was so bad a couple of times. I was the one who nursed your older sister through two—no, three—years of serious illness. And when your brother Bernard had that blood poisoning and when he came through that accident years ago, I was there. I was there in the hospital with your family, I was there in your home a number of times, and I was here in this office for a dozen other things. Routine and sometimes special problems."

He stopped to clear his throat. "You family has survived more than its share of stresses as I look back, Jeanie, but this? This one is different. Can you tell me what's wrong, Jeanie? What's bothering you inside? What's really happening?"

The size of the lump in my throat was very deceiving. Just when I thought it was big enough to obstruct words and tears, it shattered unexpectedly, like a powerless floodgate against them both, and the wracking waves surged out.

For what seemed like endless moments I sobbed and sobbed, my young hands pressed instinctively against my face. "Doctor," I cried, "I don't even know what's happening anymore. Everything's coming apart at home. And I mean *everything*."

"Relax, honey," Doctor Bradford assured. His long arm was stretched across my back, and his hand squeezed my shoulder so tightly it hurt.

"It used to be real bad before Mom filed for divorce last year, but now it's awful. Fight. Fight. Fight. When it's quiet I just sit and wait for the explosion to begin all over again. Mornings or nights. Especially on weekends. *Seems like forever it's been going on. Feels like it'll never end. My dad . . . my dad——*"

"Shh," the good doctor interjected among my wails. "Shh." The fold of his arm became the solid fortress for my heaving shoulders.

"There's no stopping him when he's mad. He will yell. And more. *He scares me so.* I go outside or I hide in my room. I can still hear him there. I get by myself and I cry and I cry. One minute I feel okay, the next so sick to my stomach I throw up. *Everything's coming apart. Everything. Sometimes I think I am, too.*"

"Oh, Jeanie," Dr. Bradford sighed and drew me closer yet. "Jeanie, I had no idea. No idea at all."

Even after several splashes of tingly cold water in the doctor's adjacent bathroom, my face was blood red. I studied it in the mirror over the porcelain sink. My nose continued to run. My eyes burned. My lips were swollen. My hair was scattered, lifeless, drab. Even with slightly blurred vision I knew I looked a mess.

I wiped my hands dry and backed away from the counter to rest on the nearby burgundy chair. It offered some support for my exhausted frame as I collected my thoughts. I had cried hard like that alone before, but never in the presence of a grownup. Especially an outsider to the family. Part of me certainly felt lighter, freer than I'd felt in months. And part of me was scared. What if Dr. Bradford told my mother the whole story? I'd rather she didn't know a thing. Sure, I knew she loved me, but she'd be mad. I was certain of it.

Even now as I stroked the chair's velvet arms her words of last week rushed back to me. "Just stay out of things, Jean," she issued sternly. "Just go to your room and stay out. None of this should bother you if you're not around to hear it." I was not one to challenge her openly, but nothing was further from the truth. The confusion at home bothered me, all right. It was eating away at me inside like a chemical acid day and night.

Time passed slowly as I sat an extra ten or fifteen minutes. Finally I checked the color of my face in the mirror and found my complexion returning to normal. The new awareness that life could resume itself gave me the added courage to walk back across the threshold of examining room C. Dr. Bradford had only now returned from another patient across the hall, and I found him by the small window recess, flashing his silver pen once more on paper.

"Jeanie," he began and looked my way, "you feel better?" He stopped for a few seconds and continued gently, "That was quite a cry."

"I feel tired," I answered, "and drained. Probably sleep like a rock tonight. But that'll be good for a change."

He jotted down a final sentence in my record file then reached for his prescription pad. "Jeanie, I've got two different medications in mind. One's going to settle your stomach a little more than the one

I gave you last month. The other pill—a little blue one—should help relax you in a kind of general way. Let's try these for the meantime and hope things settle down at home very soon."

"I pray for it daily," I whispered. "Really I do."

Dr. Bradford tore off the paper slips and handed them to me. "See that your mother gets these filled right away. Tonight. Or tomorrow."

"Speaking of my mother, Doctor," I mentioned awkwardly. "Well, could you please not tell her anything? Please? At least not yet? Please? She wouldn't understand. Sometimes she thinks I'm faking everything just to get out of work at home or going to school. Please? Please don't tell her."

The good doctor scratched his chin and reflected. "All right, for the time being. Let's see how this medicine helps first."

There was a long pause when neither of us spoke. I was too relieved to say anything.

"Jeanie, I want you to know I'm concerned about you and I'm concerned about your family. Do you understand?"

Embarrassed, I looked away from his stare and offered the only response I could give. "Think so."

"Are you going to be okay now?"

"I feel a little better. I need to get some sleep, that's all."

"I'd like you to come back in a few weeks. Around the first of next month. I want to check on how you're doing."

"Sure," I answered, "it'll give me something to look forward to . . . you know . . . in case things get bad. At least I can talk with you about it."

"Good," he replied in a firm, consenting tone of voice. He gave my hand a quick squeeze.

I tried to smile but failed, and I reached for my little brown purse. "I guess I'll see you later," I said.

"Better not forget your book," he reminded.

"Oh, yeah." I picked up *The Scarlet Letter,* opened it randomly, and stuffed the prescription papers inside. We both nodded one last time and I turned into the corridor.

On the other side of the hallway door I was surprised to find the waiting room completely empty. I temporarily detoured from the path to the exit and glanced up at the wall clock in the nurses' station. I wondered how long I'd been in the office. Seemed like hours and hours.

"Oh, Jeanie?" the friendly woman in white called from behind me.

"Your mother just now ran out to the car to turn off her parking lights. Here it is half past five and already dusk outside. I love autumn but I sure hate to see the days get shorter."

I nodded my head in silent agreement.

"I bet if you hurry you can save her a trip back in," the nurse continued.

I must have looked puzzled because she added, "Your mother? Out back in the parking lot?"

"Oh," I said. "Right."

"See you in a couple weeks," she stated and waved good-bye.

I waved too and walked away from her to the shiny clear office doors. My left palm was firmly pressed on the aluminum handle when I realized I had forgotten something. Something important.

Here again, I stood by the familiar aquarium. My eyes quickly scanned from one corner of the tank to the other. From the surface of the water down to the thousand color chips on the bottom. There were the goldfish. The zebra circle, sporting round and round. Even some other tropical varieties I'd failed to notice an hour earlier. But no little red jewel fish.

I walked to the other side of the tank. Still no spotted jewel. Cautiously I touched two fingers under the water line to examine the brownish green strands of algae. They swayed gently one way, then another. No, the tiny crimson fish was not hidden there. It was gone. Taken. Probably very sick. Or very dead.

"But it was so pretty, pretty red," I pondered. *"So pretty."*

A tear emerged in the corner of one tired eye, and I dashed it away. Then I took a deep breath and headed straight for the thick glass doors.

2

Hot Seat

IT WAS HARD—even impossible—to be contented at twelve years of age. While at home during the hours of uneasy calm or more frequent storms, I often dreamed that better pastures awaited me in school. And while at school I fancied that safer, tranquil worlds existed for me back home. The truth is, I was insecure wherever I was—no matter how I appeared on the surface. The truth is, wanting to be somewhere else was a game I played to pass the time. Quite frankly it kept me going. It was called escape. Wishful thinking. Survival.

There was only one place I dreaded being more than at home or at school and that was *en route*. In the car. My personal hot seat. No one ever gave it that name. No brothers or sisters or mother or father had ever pointed to the family car and announced, "Hey, Jeanie! Right there it is. That's your hot seat!" I guess it only seemed like one because I could never, never win there. It was in the car that I learned shame. It was in the car that I seemed trapped. It was in the car that I felt most alone and abandoned.

The cold, rainy November morning that all these emotions exploded to the surface was a Friday. School classes had been canceled because of teachers' meetings, and initially I was home, like all red-blooded children, rejoicing. Mother had been called unexpectedly into her volunteer work and my brother and sister already were scattered in neighborhood activities, so the great big empty house was left for my father and me to share. I didn't envision we would spend much time together, though. Not on a week day. My father held a midnight factory job and he was forced to use his mornings and afternoons for sleep.

During the nine o'clock hour I puttered about the house. While I munched breakfast I enjoyed several minutes of television, but turned off the set when the exercise lady demonstrated an endless string of leg splits. Left. Right. Left. Right. It hurt just to watch. Next I fiddled with the kitchen radio and sketched a drawing on the back of an old piece of paper as I listened. It wasn't a bad horse for a first try. Finally I went to my bedroom, changed from my pajamas into blue jeans, and decided to jump back into bed. Perhaps I'd clean my cluttered room today after a quick nap.

My head rested a long time on the small white pillow. If I held my breath and listened intently I could hear the rain tap against the roof above me. It was comforting. I lay still and thought how peaceful this moment seemed. Quiet in the house. Calmer within since I began taking Dr. Bradford's medication two weeks ago. I felt drowsy more often, but at least I could relax. At least I could sleep better at night.

"Here, kitty, kitty," I called into the morning silence. "Here, Popcorn. Come on up, kitty."

Like always, my big black cat tore up the wooden steps, into my room, and launched straight to my bed at the mention of his name. Sometimes I figured he was the only true listener I had.

"Oh, Popcorn," I whispered and scratched his head. "How are you doing today, huh?"

As was his habit, he crawled upon my stomach and began to knead at the already snagged blanket. He must have been in heaven today because he purred with a loud, steady thrum and drooled a little at my stroking.

"I forgot to feed you, Popcorn," I chatted. "Where were you this morning anyway? Want to go back down for a bowl of milk and food? Huh, boy?" I waited like he could really answer. "Well, Popcorn? What is it? Now or later?"

A creaking sound on the steps made me cease my silly monologue. Even Popcorn cocked his head sideways toward the stairwell to listen. It couldn't be Bernie or Christine. They'd have made more noise and they'd never have come back home so soon. No, it was my father. I reckoned he wanted something important because he hardly ever visited me on the second floor.

"I heard you up here," he said and walked through the archway entrance. He was bare chested, dressed only in his gray work pants. "I got to go across town to get a part for the car. I think you should come with me." My dad never asked anything in his whole life. I knew it was really a command to go, and I, the youngest in the family, was powerless to resist.

I said nothing at first. I didn't like this business of traveling alone with my dad because he had a temper. A bad temper. An unpredictable temper. The kind of temper that might explode now, on the spot, if I showed opposition. And I admit I didn't like traveling in that car, either. It seemed to me like it was always breaking down. Always.

"How soon are you going to leave?" I asked.

"Few minutes."

"I got to feed Popcorn first."

"Hurry up about it. That cat gets fatter every blessed day."

"Do you . . . do you think . . . can I take Popcorn?"

"You and that black cat," he uttered in disgust and threw out one muscular arm. "I don't care. Just don't let it climb all over everything."

Granted, Popcorn didn't offer the lasting kind of security I needed, but he was better than nothing. Caring for him in the car would give me something to do. It would enable me to handle better the deafening quiet or pronounced rage of my father, whichever extreme might occur in his presence.

Reluctantly I dragged myself out of bed and grabbed for my shoes below. In the short time it took to tie the laces I noticed a tightening in my stomach. My throat even constricted. Why was my father still standing here—silent, arms folded—watching me? I was hurrying as fast as I could.

Popcorn followed close to my heels. We left my bedroom and together brushed by Father into the dark hallway. I knew better than to respond to his brittle reminder, "Hustle it!"

"It's just you and me, kitty," I whispered into Popcorn's ear while I stroked his head and watched him eat. "Why did they have to cancel school today, huh? Huh, Popcorn? Well, at least I have you."

Father didn't say another word. He just towered over me and cleared his raspy throat. That was his way of telling me he was ready to leave. From where I knelt on the floor beside Popcorn's feeding dish, Father looked like a huge machine—terrible and immovable. A giant!

I quickly glanced down at my blue checked jacket, rejoined the unzipped ends, and then heaved Popcorn up to my shoulder. "Ready," I said.

There was no verbal answer. Only a pointed arm toward the side door exit. Only the rattle of keys hitting keys in a powerfully strong hand.

It occurred to me as I blinked against the misty rain that I had meant to grab a book and my little purse on the way out, but there was no time left. Taking Popcorn was in itself an unusual victory, and I didn't want to push my luck with another thirty-second delay, for Father was now locking the house door behind us.

"Thank God for you, kitty," I sighed under my breath.

Father and I walked to the car without speaking. I used one of my arms to shield Popcorn from the falling rain while I opened the passenger door to our old green Ford with the other. I slid onto the seat and slammed the door hard behind me. Popcorn jerked in fear from the reverberation of sound. "Sorry, boy. It's okay," I said. "Didn't mean to give you a scare."

Next Father's door fanned wide open and a gust of November air whirled past him toward me. "Yuck," I said, "what's that smell in here?"

"What are you talking about?" he replied.

"Vinegar. I think it's vinegar. Strong vinegar. Can't you smell it?"

"Oh, it's just your imagination."

I inhaled deeply. "Really, it's vinegar. Smells sour or something."

He forced his door shut with both hands. "You got the best imagination of any kid your age, you know? Can't say much else, but you do got that."

If there was anything that bred self-doubts in my twelve-year-old frame it was this business of my imagination. Once my English teacher said my imagination was the ace up my sleeve in writing the little papers I sometimes turned in for class. She smiled when she told me and made me feel real good. But my father? My mother? When they said I had an imagination it sounded like a curse. Like I didn't know the difference between the truth and a made-up story. Like I couldn't think or feel or see things for myself.

"Thought sure it was vinegar," I uttered quietly.

"Well, it's not so shut up," he concluded.

Once the ignition key was firmly in place the engine ground and ground with unconnected sputters. Four tries and it still wouldn't start. Five. Six. I clutched Popcorn against my jacket while Father jumped out of the old green car and raised the wet hood. *What was it now?*

Even though delays like this one seemed to be the typical way our journeys were interrupted, I never learned to accept them gracefully. At least not inside where I felt panicky and stranded. It was always something in this hot seat of a car, and fixing it was a kind of ritual that followed us wherever we went. If it wasn't the fan belt, it was the water pump. If it wasn't a bald, flat tire, it was an empty gas tank. A corroded wire. A broken gasket. An uncharging generator. And on and on it went. I knew the problems well, I just never got used to them.

Today, even with the car windows rolled tight against the November drizzle, I could hear Father's profanity from under the hood. His words exploded with the steady beat of fireworks. This was not going to be a good day for either of us. I could tell. And my stomach was already keeping score.

"Popcorn," I spoke into his dark black ears, "is it just my luck or does this car *never* work? I hate this car. Hear me? I hate it. I hate it."

I stared up at the house through rain-dotted windows as Father sat behind the steering wheel and continued his nasty monologue. The dreary house looked empty and shiveringly cold drenched in the liquid spray, but more than anything I longed to go back to it and retreat from my father and from his car.

A seventh try. An eighth. I couldn't actually tell if I was relieved or dismayed when the engine turned over and roared into being on the ninth turn of the key. Perhaps if the old car hadn't started I could have returned inside for the day. That would have brought relief! Instead we pulled out the drive, and I found myself praying, "Dear God, please get me home safe and sound. Please?"

It suited me fine that we didn't converse during the first miles of our excursion because there was one specific rule I discovered a long time ago: I was safest with my father if I kept quiet. The less I said, the better we got along. I didn't necessarily like the lonely, submissive existence I led around him, but I figured it was the best way to survive. It kept me in his good graces and out of trouble most of the time.

"What are you doing over there?" Father asked, turning onto the northbound expressway ramp. Popcorn dug his claws into my left knee to brace himself on the car's steady incline, and I winced a little in pain.

"Nothing," I replied. "Just petting Popcorn and keeping him warm on my lap."

"You and that cat," he scowled. "You and that damn black cat."

Even on a good day I doubted if our old green Ford could match the sixty-miles-per-hour speed limit posted for freeway travel. Usually cars passed us. That's why I was surprised when my father reduced his speed in the right-hand lane behind what appeared to be a shiny white Buick. Its illuminated red tail lights flickered on and off in front of us as we followed for three or four minutes. It was a newer car model but it must have been experiencing engine difficulty the way it slowed down.

I heard Father mutter something under his breath about women drivers and I looked through the foggy window ahead to find my own clue to the driver's identity. Maybe I could spot a feathery hat. Or long curled hair. Or a big fat cigar if it happened to be a man. I squinted against the flip flap of wiper blades but it was no use. Between the dripping rain and foggy windows I couldn't tell for sure, and I doubted if Father could tell either.

"You think if she's going to poke around she could use the side streets," he growled and intentionally moved closer to the car in front of us. "They ought to just shoot women drivers and get it over with."

I drew out one hand from Popcorn's warm side and braced it against the dusty gray dashboard. It looked like we'd hit. "But . . . but what if she stops all of a sudden?"

Father honked the horn and jolted our car up against the Buick's bumper on purpose. Bang! "She shouldn't be on here. *Women!*"

My hands dripped with sweat. My stomach twisted. "But what if she's got car trouble or can't see too well? Can't you just go around her?" I asked while Father surged ahead a second time. I braced my feet against the floorboards, held onto Popcorn, and continued, "I don't understand. *What's hitting her bumper supposed to do?*"

When I noticed fearful excitement in my voice I realized it was time to get quiet. I was afraid I'd already said too much, and I was worried about what might happen if Father continued his driving stunts. What was he trying to prove by jerking us back and forth? What? That he was a big man on the highway? What?

After a fourth hit Father finally dropped back to switch lanes. He'd had his fun. When he roared by the side of the big white Buick he held his hand to the horn, waved to the driver with his other, and laughed. I was too humiliated to look. I slumped down and pretended to fuss with Popcorn.

My father smacked my shoulder. "You worry too much, kid," he chuckled. "You know that?" Next to my imagination, my parents' second favorite criticism of me had to do with my worrying. Only this time they had me: I did worry a lot. Experiences like this one had taught me how to do it and *do it well.*

"Yes, sir," I agreed and prayed the discussion would end there.

At least twenty drivers passed us on the wet freeway in the following ten minutes of travel. Not one of the drivers—male or female—hit our back bumper. Not one of them honked a horn or waved in triumph. I noticed, but I wondered if my father noticed. I wondered if he even cared.

"Eh, how soon will we be there?" I asked with a phony touch of cheer in my voice. My stomach was issuing terrible pains now. I was finding it hard to swallow. How I wished I were back home or at my desk in school!

"Pretty soon," he answered. "What the—" He stopped in mid-sentence and glared at the dashboard instrument panel. I looked down, too, and discovered the water temperature gauge pointed directly under the letter *H.* Even I knew it should be in the middle between the cold and hot markers. Father instinctively took his foot from the gas pedal and flipped on his right turn signal. We then coasted to the side of the road.

"Dear God," I thought to myself. "Here on the freeway? Trouble on the freeway in this rainy mess?"

Father had no sooner locked the gear stick in park than we saw the streaming lines of vapor shoot out from the cracks and vents on the engine hood. He quickly grabbed for his silver door handle. He was gone. I couldn't distinguish exact words this time on account of the traffic noise and rain around us, but I knew my father was furious by the discharge of syllables coming from his flaming red face. Through the front window I watched him wrap his large handkerchief around one clenched fist and lean forward to release the hood latch. That's all it took. White steam billowed out from underneath.

For a few minutes I sat in the middle of our steam shower. The boiling water from our radiator mixed with the chilly downpour and made an awful sight. At a time like this it was strange that I thought of my science teacher. He'd be so proud of my field experience—actually witnessing clouds in the making!

I decided to join my father, who was still outside the car. Maybe he could end my panic by telling me everything was okay. Maybe I could feel more secure just standing next to him. I only knew I was scared inside. Really scared.

When I prodded open the door with the heel of my shoe it never occurred to me to leave Popcorn on the seat behind. I knew about loneliness in the car, and I knew my cat would be better off with me in the rain than by himself inside the tin shell. It was cold and empty there. I scooped him in my hands and stepped out. Popcorn arched and twisted against the fold of my arms, but I was unaware of his struggles. I was too busy trying to cope with my own.

"What's wrong?" I shouted to Father.

No answer.

"Do you know what's wrong? Can you fix it?" I reiterated, breathless and worried.

Still no answer.

Color and anger and fatigue bled across Father's face, and for one isolated moment in time I caught something of his own pathetic frustration. "Dad?" I said.

Half man and half insane he lunged toward the exposed engine and grabbed hold of the boiling radiator hose. With all the strength in him, he jerked upward, then outward, ripping the rubber tube from both its metal connectors. He screamed a smattering of words—none of which I could understand—and flung the black hose skyward with unrestrained force. I opened my mouth and stared upward. Our tubing disappeared in the hazy distance, somewhere down the steep hill beyond the guardrail. It might just as well have soared a million miles away for all the good it would do us now.

"Dad?" I called.

I had never seen him so irritated with the car. "What are you doing?" I yelled and swabbed the rain from my brow with a blue checked sleeve.

He did not look like my words reached his ears. Enraged, he deliberately crashed his right fist against the oily surface of the too hot engine. A bloody river spread from between his fingers and palm, and he jerked his hand back to his chest in pain.

"For God's sake," I cried out. *"Are you crazy?"*

The look on his face was one of total anger. Total fury. He first slammed down the hood with dynamite force. Then he whirled my way and poised that bloody fist inches from my nose. I was too terrified to move. I closed my eyes, waiting for the striking blow, and covered Popcorn as best I could with my shaking arms.

"If you're going to do it, *do it now,*" I begged above the noise of cars and distant thunder.

My heart raced uncontrollably. My stomach was on fire. I trembled. In the seconds that followed I was astonished to find that no calloused hand met my wet cheek. I agonized a minute longer in darkness. Finally I opened my eyes to discover that Father was twenty or more yards from me along the cement pavement. He was walking away.

"Wait!" I shrieked against the falling rain and ran toward him. "Wait! Where are you going?"

He turned around and commanded in his huge voice, "Go to the car!"

"But," I protested, "but where are you going? Take me with you this time! Please don't leave me! I don't even know where we are! At least tell me where you're going!"

He continued walking backward long enough to scream, *"Get back in the damn car! You hear me?"*

"Don't leave me, Father, don't leave me!" I cried. "Please let me come. I won't cause any trouble. Honest!"

In a streak of cruelty he turned his back to me and broke into a run. His legs pumped angrily and I knew I would never catch up to him now. "Oh, God," I wept aloud as the cars flashed by. "Oh, God. Oh, God."

The noise of rain was everywhere. I stood dazed in its foreboding melody. I was soaked. Numb. For a long, long time I let the drops sting against my face and mingle with the already present tears. Both splashed straight down in parallel paths over my flushed cheeks.

There was nothing in my tear-showered vision except the chasm of rain that separated us. I could not guess how long ago I had seen the final glimpse of my father. Five minutes? Ten? More? I couldn't tell when he'd return or how. Even, in his present state, if he'd bother to come back for me. Was I worth his effort?

Popcorn wrestled in my rigid arms, spitting and clawing for his freedom. "Kitten," I wept and pulled him close to my neck. "Kitty, I'm sorry. I'm so sorry. We'll go back. I'll dry you off."

On the lonely journey back to the car I brushed my clammy hands against the damp tufts of Popcorn's fur. My tight grasp was too much for his struggling black body, and I heard him bellow out thin frail cries of his own.

"Shh, boy," I sniffled. "You're safe with me. I won't leave you. I could never leave you."

I thought it was for his security that I clung so dearly to Popcorn in the rain, but I was wrong. It was for mine. That black cat was the only thing I valued in all my world. I needed him to cuddle. I needed him to love. And sometimes I needed him for my own soundness of mind. Today more than ever.

I stumbled slowly along the side of the freeway, trying to avoid the broken pieces of glass and roadside debris. Cars blinked their yellow beams at me as they flew by, but only one car came to a halt on the berm where I walked. It was a brown sedan driven by a gray-haired woman. She cracked the passenger's window a few inches, leaned across her front seat, and asked, "You all right, honey?"

All right? What is *all right?* I wondered to myself. Is *all right* losing this morning's breakfast cereal, sick to my stomach, only moments ago? Is *all right* the feeling of humiliation I sensed in that horrible car or here beside the road? Is *all right* the fear inside? The exhaustion?

"Honey?" she repeated.

"I . . . I don't know," I told the kind woman in my quivering voice. I figured there wasn't anything she could do. I didn't know where I was, where Father was, or where the store was that could sell us automobile parts. "That green car right over there," I shouted toward her window and pointed a few feet away. "It's ours. It . . . it broke down and I'm supposed to stay there. I guess my dad will come back soon as he can. I hope so."

I thought I had my panic under control until she said, "You look awful scared. Well, you best get inside your car. You lock those doors. Hear?"

"Lock doors . . . right," I repeated mechanically.

She began to roll up the window when it occurred to me to ask. "Say, lady? If . . . if you see a man walking further down—he's not real tall, got a brown coat on and gray pants, he hurt his hand—well, maybe you can give him a lift to the next exit or something? You think?"

"I'll keep my eye out for him. Now you better scoot to your car before you get pneumonia. And lock those doors, honey. Lock 'em real tight."

"Yeah," I said as I watched her pull away.

"Popcorn," I called and began to sob all over again, "why does this kind of stuff have to happen to us? Why? If only Bernie were here or Christine. Even Peter, if Dad would let him come back home. But no, it's just you and me. Just you and me, kitty."

My fingers felt for the door handle of our car and I crawled onto the front seat. I was tired. So defeated. I set Popcorn by my left thigh and, before shutting the door, pulled off my wet jacket to cover him. It was all I had to offer. It was my little extravagance of affection.

"There, there, boy," I said. I coughed hard and stroked Popcorn with one of the empty blue sleeves. "Is it chilly in here for you? Oh, Popcorn, what would I do without you? I don't love anybody but you. Nobody, kitten. You're the only one. You listen when I talk. You come to me. You never make me feel bad. You're the only one I love. Just you."

There wasn't anything to do but wait. There was no book to read. No paper to draw or write on. No purse with nicknacks, even, and no medication to ease my stomach cramps. There was nothing but Popcorn, me, and this detestable hot seat of a car.

I readjusted myself on the worn air cushion and turned sideways so my back leaned fully against the passenger door and both legs ran the complete length of the seat. Little Popcorn was too tired to clean and too wet to care, and he preferred the resting place of my lap. I liked him there, too. At least he was something in the way of security in this dreary mess.

"Well, look at that, kitty," I said and moved one foot toward the steering wheel. "He forgot to take the keys. Maybe he'll come back for us after all. What do you think?"

I quieted and folded my arms for warmth. With nothing else to do, my eyes followed the steering column downward to the darkness of pedals below and hanging wires. I noticed the floor mat was nearly caked with muddy bootprints. Particles of dead autumn leaves were crushed and scattered there also. I spotted a quarter by Father's door. And something else. Something curved round with a touch of shine.

"Sorry, kitty," I said, finagling my body to reach beyond him without too much discomfort. The hump in the middle of the floor didn't make my work any easier. "What in the world is this?" I asked.

I jerked and pulled against the wiry springs and produced a bottle from beneath Father's seat. It wasn't like any soda pop container I'd seen before. This one was rounder. Like a tall glass cylinder with a long slim neck. There was an inch or two of tea-colored liquid sloshing inside. It looked nasty. And there was the metal cap that first drew my attention. The green paper strip glued over part of it puzzled me.

I decided to unscrew the top. "Yuck!" I blared. "That's it, Popcorn. That's the vinegar smell I was talking about when we got inside the car this morning. Does it ever stink!" I squinted my eyes. Only then did I turn the bottle around to see the foil label. Part of it was torn off. What remained read: Lord York's Whiskey, 90 proof, one fifth.

I knew it couldn't be Mother's. She was opposed to drinking because I'd heard her say it time and time before. Even in her conversations with Father. And she'd never think of hiding something like this under the seat. But Father? Now that was a different story. I *could* see him tucking this away. Getting it out. Drinking. It would certainly explain a lot of things to me. Things like his roller-coaster temper, the scent of his breath when he got home from work, his habit of swearing, and those frequent trips to the garage.

"That's just great, Popcorn," I said and replaced the thin golden cap. "I don't even want to touch this. He'll kill me if he finds it in my hands." I was careful to duplicate the same angle from which the container was removed, and then I leaned back over the edge of the seat and forced the bottle home.

"Do you hate this place as much as I do, kitty?" I spoke into his pointed, attentive ears. He responded with a faint whisp of sound. He was content. He listened.

"The memories here . . . ," I said and looked around.

How could I forget the countless times I was left alone in the car while Father and Mother shopped at stores and ran their errands? At least with Bernie or Christine or Peter stuck here with me it was bearable. I was their little sister and they sometimes played games with me and talked with me and told me jokes. They helped me forget where I was.

"I remember one time," I told Popcorn, "before you were born. Maybe six or seven years ago. I was sitting on the seat right where we are now, only in the car before this. Downtown. Of course, Dad took off and left me here. I fell asleep I was so bored. Woke up scared, forgot where I was and all that, and wet my pants. Didn't mean to, Popcorn, didn't mean to. I was just scared and it was getting dark. Couldn't see him anywhere. I cried, cried, cried. Then when he finally came he laughed at me. Thought it was funny. Called me a big baby. Then I *really* cried. I never felt so ashamed in my whole life, kitty. The teasing and jokes. I could have died. Wanted to.

"And there were other times, Popcorn. Other times in here I can still see today. Like what was said during arguments. Or during the breakdowns. I mean it, Popcorn, you're a captive audience in here. And how I hated to rush to their 'Hurry up or we'll leave you' threats.

In gas station bathrooms, or stores, or dropping off things here or there, I *flew* just because I was afraid they'd pull out without me. And I already told you about the time I was sitting right back there, right in the corner pocket, and got it for crying. 'Grow up and shut up,' he told me. Boy, did that sting. Except when I'm with you, Popcorn, I learned to cry inside after that one."

I grew still and groped for a long-forgotten Kleenex I discovered in the fold of the seat. It fell apart in my hands when I spread out its four corners for use, but I managed to salvage enough to blow my nose.

I leaned my head all the way back against the glass, drew in a huge breath, and closed my eyes. "Popcorn, do you know why I was even born? Huh, boy? I don't. Really I don't. Seriously. Seems like I don't belong anywhere." I stopped a moment, rubbed my moist, tired eyes, and yawned again. "You? You belong with me. But where, Popcorn, where do I belong? Where? Do you know?"

Unexpectedly I was roused from my deep slumber by the surge of engine power as our old green Ford moved into third gear. I blinked my eyes hard and tried to focus. What time was it? My feet were now draped over the center hump instead of on the seat where I left them. Sleepy, I stretched out my legs and coughed and coughed. I was relieved to see that Popcorn was here, curled by my side in a tight ball on my drier-than-before jacket. And Father was back. His hand was loosely wrapped in a white bandage. It had no professional touch like tape or a clasp; probably he had wound the cloth around and around his hand himself.

"You were sleeping like a log," he told me.

I didn't answer, but noticed my father's coat draped over my chest and shoulders.

"You were cold," he stated in a low voice. "Ice cold."

I turned my head to look out my side window. The sky was pale blue with hints of gray, and it had stopped raining. If the storm was over, I wondered, why did I still feel like I was falling apart? Why did I feel like I'd walked through a dream—a horrible dream—and had barely come out on the other side?

"You should have locked the doors," Father added gently. His volume was not booming as before. He was in control now. Quieter. I suppose he was apologetic in his own way.

He motioned to the dashboard ledge and said, "There's a sandwich in the bag for you. It's after lunch." I coughed again and stared out the right door window. The way my stomach felt I might not eat for the rest of my life.

Father seemed fidgety. "That lousy hose had a crack in it. I guess from age or something. A guy down at Maxie's helped me out and gave me a lift back. Only took a few minutes to put it on and add the water."

I chose not to respond. All I wanted to do was forget this day, forget this car, forget everything.

"We're . . . we're on our way home now," he said. "Be there in a little bit."

Home? Going home? I wanted to cry. I wanted to go home, all right, and run to my room, lock the door tight, and never, ever come out. How I hated it here. Here in this car. Panicked, I continued to stare at the moving landscape around us. I knew something deep inside of me had changed that November noon. Something had snapped. I had crossed an imaginary line and I would never go back. I did not want to go back. I think the line was trust. Trust in my father.

"You're . . . you're awful quiet," he stated.

Silence.

"It wasn't that bad, now was it?"

Silence.

"Oh, come on."

Silence.

"Can *I* help it if the car breaks down?"

Silence.

"You worry too much, kid. You know that?"

Silence.

"Aw, the hell with you. The hell with all of you."

There was no reply to come during the long, lonely drive home. All that met our ears was the clickety-clack roar of the old Ford engine.

3

The Family of God

IT SEEMED TO ME like my family was born for church the way we spent so much time there. I'm not complaining. No, no, no. A lot of fond memories emerged from our attendance. Up until the last few years, when Father gradually pulled away and stayed at home more than he went, church had provided the one sense of unity we lacked in other areas. It gave us a purpose. It brought us together peacefully.

For the most part I liked church. I don't mean the morning worship service, although there was something comforting about it, or Sunday night fellowship, or the prayer meetings we attended every Wednesday. I'm referring to Sunday school and the other activities that corralled us youngsters together under one roof. Sometimes, I admit, we got away with murder when supervision was low and attendance was high, or when everybody's Dear Aunt Bertha came in for story time and smothered us with her uncritical love, or when the lessons and recreation were just plain *poor*. All things considered, though, I liked it there.

I felt safe at church. I felt wanted. And because I faithfully brought my Bible, memorized verses in a flash, never missed a Sunday, and recited God's fourfold plan of salvation at the drop of anyone's hat (this began for me in the third grade), I felt needed. When the going got tough and the teachers didn't know what else to do, they could always count on me to read or recite or pray and get us back on the track. I didn't mind. It made me feel special.

During my seventh grade year I was under the sometimes not-so-wise leadership of Eleanor Fishwangler. Among her many rules, she insisted we students call her Miss Eleanor. Only Miss Eleanor. I think it had something to do with all the deliberate, attention-getting variations that kids invented for her last name. Variations I wouldn't dare repeat. Miss Eleanor was a middle-aged spinster, strong-willed, and always smelled of lilacs.

Like the minister and just about everyone else I knew at church, Miss Eleanor saw things in the world as clearly black and white. You were either very good or you were very bad. You were totally saved or you were totally lost. All or nothing on every issue in life. No in-between. The very mention of gray shades spelled heresy. People would pray for you until you came from your darkness back into the light. People like Miss Eleanor. People who took their faith seriously.

Now that the Christmas season was fading away with the reality of January's arrival, Miss Eleanor returned to our regular book of junior high lessons. One of these units was meant to show how believers work and fit together in the same Christian body. "Next week when you come back," Miss Eleanor told the dozen of us in my seventh grade class, "be sure to bring snapshots of your family members with you. I've got something special in mind. It's kind of a different angle to our family of God unit." She even reminded us again individually on our way out of the room. "Remember the pictures! Remember the pictures!"

It dawned on me as I got dressed for church the following Sunday morning that I'd forgotten to collect my photographs during the week for our class project. I wasn't sure exactly what Miss Eleanor had in mind by asking us to bring them, but I didn't want to let her down. I knew she would be counting on me.

"Mom, where's our old box of photos?" I asked, trying to keep my voice down so I wouldn't disturb Father's sleep. "I'm supposed to take a couple with me for Sunday school."

Mother put on her winter coat and searched for her brown gloves in the pocket. "Oh, let's see," she replied. "No, they're not up there anymore . . . try the hall closet. Don't mix them up when you finger through them. And hurry. We're leaving soon."

She stopped long enough to ask Bernie, who passed in front of us for the bathroom, to please clear off the snow from the car windows, and she finished by telling me I had three minutes to grab whatever I needed and scramble outside.

"Let's see," I mused and flashed through the black and white photo collection. "That's Mom and Dad . . . Peter . . . There's Christine's . . . oh, yeah, Bernie. Oops, where's Popcorn? The one of him outside on Christmas day? I know it's here somewhere." I sifted and rooted through every corner of the shoebox. Luckily, just as Mother honked the horn in the drive, I pulled out the picture of my inkspot kitty buried in a huge December snowdrift. "Popcorn, you're so cute," I said and threw the photographs inside the leather jacket of my Bible for safekeeping. I shoved the box in the closet and hastened to join Mother, Christine, and Bernie in the car.

What a treat it was to have Mother behind the wheel, Bernie beside me, and Christine in front. Even on their worst days I'd take the company of these three a thousand times over Father's. And it was such a delight to ride in the second-hand car Mother bought last month for transportation now that she had a new job. The car was probably eight years old, but it worked. So far it hadn't broken down once for us.

Because there was only a light dusting of snow that covered the roads, we made good time on our way to church. In fact, we arrived about ten minutes ahead of most people. I burst out of the car, headed for the stained-glass doors, and peeled off my coat. Next I went to find Peter and waited a couple minutes, but he wasn't in the empty classroom of high schoolers he taught. When he didn't come and didn't come I decided to rush downstairs and visit with Miss Eleanor in the remaining time. Hopefully I could catch Peter after the worship service.

"Well, hi there, Jeanie!" Miss Eleanor greeted when I came through the door. I caught her in the middle of writing lyrics for today's songs on the blackboard.

"Hi, Miss Eleanor. Guess what? I remembered the pictures just like you asked. Thought of them on my way out the door a few minutes ago."

"I knew you would," she said. Miss Eleanor was always confident in my abilities and often told me so.

"Got anything you want me to do?" I asked. "Straighten chairs? Pass out books or anything?"

"Thanks for asking, honey, but I think everything's taken care of. Did you learn your memory work for today to get your sticker on the poster?"

"Sure I did. I want a perfect record," I beamed.

"Then let's hear you say your verses," Miss Eleanor challenged. "Without looking."

"Okay," I agreed. "Want me to first tell you where they're from?"

She smiled. "Of course, Jeanie. Begin there."

I turned my face away from the board and looked down. "Okay, here goes. They're found in First Corinthians twelve, beginning with verse twenty-five. 'There should be no division in the body, but that the members should have the same care for one another. And if one member suffers, all the members suffer with it; if one member is honored, all the members rejoice with it.'"

I stopped for her positive recognition and realized I'd forgotten to quote the final line. "Oh, yeah. Verse twenty-seven says, 'Now you are Christ's body, and individually members of it.' Now I'm through."

"Very good, Jeanie," she said. "Very good indeed."

"Is that why you had us bring pictures? To show we're many members or something?"

"Right. I figured that would help make the point that we're all one big happy family. Your family, my family, we all make up the family of God."

"You really believe that, Miss Eleanor?"

"Why sure I do," she stated.

"You going to make us pass these around?" I wondered aloud and reached into my Bible to produce the handful of pictures. "I didn't stop to pick out the best ones; I only took the first I could find."

"No, I didn't think of passing them around. They'd get smudged that way. Instead I thought it would be good if every child took a turn, held up the pictures, and told us something about each family member. Their hobbies. Interests. Whatever. Before they're finished I'd like the children to talk about love in their family and how important love is to getting along."

My heart was beginning to sink. "Really?" I stated. "We got to stand up there?" I motioned to the frail wooden lectern in front of our classroom. "And talk about how important love is?"

"No, we're not going to use the podium. I think we'll all just sit in our sharing circle to talk. How does that sound?"

I was still dazed. "And we've got to say something about our families? Each member?" I asked again. I didn't like this idea of hers. I didn't like it *at all.* The last thing I needed or wanted was to have the spotlight on my family and me. Even for a minute. Even in the secure womb of my church. How in the world could I give a rundown on our family life? Or worse, our family love? I didn't think I could handle it. Not out loud. Not in front of the others.

"This picture idea would be a nice way to get better acquainted with each other, don't you think, Jeanie?" Miss Eleanor posed. "We'll spend about half an hour sharing and then I've got some Scriptures on the family of God I want to close with. It will be a nice change of pace from our usual lessons where I do all the talking."

I began to stutter. "But . . . but what if someone . . . well, doesn't want to go along . . . along and talk in the circle?"

"Oh, come on. You?" She looked so surprised.

"Well, yeah, for instance. Let's say I didn't want to."

"You've spoken in here lots of times, Jeanie. You aren't getting shy on us are you?" She laughed a little when she mentioned the word shy.

"No . . . no."

"Then you'll do fine, and don't be so modest! I'm sure you'll think of lots of nice, interesting things to say. Everyone already knows you come from a good strong family in this church. Your folks have been members here for years and years. Even before me. And they've done a wonderful job raising your brothers, your sister, you. Jeanie, you don't have to be bashful to tell us how much they mean to you. Or how much you mean to them. I think it's admirable you're all so close. Just relax and tell the truth."

Close? We're all so close? Tell how much I mean to them? Tell the truth? Expose how worthless, how in the way, how hopeless I feel? How helpless? She sure wasn't making this easy. "I . . . I don't think you understand," I said and shifted from foot to foot. "I just don't want to do it, that's all. I've got another cold and I . . . I don't feel up to talking today."

"But you sound fine to me," she contradicted.

"I mean go through the pictures and all that stuff." I moved my arm in a circular pattern to show the arrangement of seats. "For them."

"Something bothering you?" she replied.

"Nothing's bothering me," I lied. "I just don't want to do it, that's all."

We were distracted when three seventh graders came running into the room. Miss Eleanor waved and shouted, "Such enthusiasm! Hi, Teddy, Sue, Mark! Better slow down, children!" Two others, Beth and Mary Lou, walked across the threshold next.

"I tell you what, Jeanie. We're about to begin in a little bit, so why don't you have a seat and rest your voice? You'll be up to par when it's your turn. It'll do all of us good to stop and appreciate the love we get. So often we take it for granted."

"But . . . but I don't think you un—" Miss Eleanor had already pulled away and was at the door to welcome other boys and girls.

The more I thought about it, the less I wanted to cooperate. I simply couldn't trust myself and what I might say concerning that vulnerable, raw area of my life. I thought fast on my feet—very fast—for ways to avoid participating. But in the short amount of time I only came up with three.

One, I could leave class now, before it began, and hide out in one of the girls' restrooms. If other kids could pull it off during Sunday school so could I. If caught I could claim I didn't feel well, which was the honest to goodness truth in light of Miss Eleanor's assignment. Second, I could stay in class and refuse to take part when it came my turn. The question is, could I handle myself calmly if everyone stared and asked why? Or teased? Could I stick to my guns?

The third option was to join in with the others and cough up some comments that sounded good and everybody expected to hear. If I wanted to go all the way, I could perjure myself on the spot and save face just like my parents had been doing outside the home for the past year or so. It seemed obvious to me that Mother and Father were *especially* on guard at church. They never said why, but I figured if they admitted their struggles then people would lose respect for them. Or they'd drop Mom and Dad as friends real fast. Or they'd be the target of gossip. I'd heard that kind of gossip in my own living room when Mr. and Mrs. Smith separated. "There's sin in their lives," Mrs. Grant told Mother. "Just plain sin. All they need is a good healthy dose of repentance and to get on with their lives!"

Since I was seated with the other children when Miss Eleanor began leading us through her favorite songs, I scrapped my idea to leave for the restroom. I didn't have favorable impressions of other kids who had resorted to that kind of "spiritual escape," as our minister had referred to it one time in a Sunday sermon. I certainly did not want to risk being numbered among them. A reputation like that would stick.

No, I decided to go to Plan B: stay, but request they pass over my turn. I would be honest and straightforward that way. If Miss Eleanor protested or if enough of the class members pressed me to share, then and only then would I move to Plan C: tell them what they wanted to hear.

When the singing was over and the offering and prayer requests had been taken care of, I knew we were getting down to the serious business of today's lesson. Miss Eleanor took only a few minutes to explain the sharing project with us. Everyone thought it was a nice idea because we seldom had discussions or got to chime in. Finally Miss Eleanor took inventory and found that Mary Lou forgot her pictures, the Baker twins missed our assignment because they were out of town last Sunday, and we had one visitor. That left seven of us, plus our teacher, who could show and tell about areas of our lives.

Miss Eleanor began with Mark, the blond-headed heartthrob of the seventh grade class. Even as she spoke his name I calculated how long until it would be my turn. If Miss Eleanor went to his right, I'd have plenty of time. If she worked to his left, I would follow Carrie, who sat next to Mark.

Mark was funny. He told us a couple jokes about his new baby brother's size and crying and his trip home from the hospital. He also pointed out how ugly little Eric seemed in the baby pictures he brought. We laughed. We agreed. Miss Eleanor interrupted to ask questions about the adjustments needed to accept a newborn into his family. What was this new baby's role with Mark and his parents? Were there drawbacks?

Then Mark mentioned some facts about the hobbies he and his father shared. He had a snapshot of the two of them fishing in Canada, and another of them washing the family car. His mother's hobby was photography, and Mark couldn't find any pictures of her to bring because she was always behind the camera.

"Love?" Mark responded to another of Miss Eleanor's questions. "Sure they love me and they mean a lot to me. Even my mother, who yells sometimes. When she was in the hospital last month with Eric . . . well, I missed her a lot. And my dad? He's always after me to get me to try harder in sports, and he'll practice with me out in the yard. I guess we like each other and it kind of goes both ways. That's all I got to say."

"That's wonderful, Mark. It's true that love goes both ways, just like you said," Miss Eleanor mentioned. How I dreaded to hear her continue, "Okay, let's move to Carrie. Carrie?" Now I knew I was only minutes away. I was feeling sicker and sicker inside.

"Carrie?" Miss Eleanor repeated a second time. "Could you give us a little something?"

Carrie's speech wasn't as exciting as Mark's. It wasn't as easy to follow, either. Carrie was an only child, born of well-to-do parents, and she wasn't too bright. She was in special classes at school, classes meant for those who had a hard time keeping pace with others their age. Sadly, we children at church always used to make fun of Carrie, but we stopped a year ago because one of our Sunday school teachers let us have it. Finally it got through our heads there was something pathetic about Carrie, and something likable once we gave her half a chance.

Carrie held up her colored photos, all professionally taken, and tried to explain that her father worked with money (he was a bank executive) and her mother was in school (she was a chemistry teacher). "Daddy's at his job and Mommy's at home when I'm done. I get to ride home on a bus. Mommy takes me in her car. I like snow. I got a shiny baton for Christmas. It's January out."

She stopped and her eyes looked like two big blue buttons. "It can bite! Red bird I saw on the ledge outside my window today. It's called a Chardennnnel! It's red! It can fly!" We assumed Carrie was done when she plopped the pictures into her lap, folded her hands, and smiled.

Miss Eleanor remarked with obvious enthusiasm, "Thank you so much, honey! Those pictures are very nice!" Carrie glowed in her teacher's praise. Miss Eleanor went on to ask, "Do you think your mother and father love you a lot, Carrie?"

"Oh, bunches!" Carrie answered. "Bunches and bunches!"

"That's very nice!" Miss Eleanor told us in her high-pitched voice.

The moment of truth had come. Everyone's eyes moved from Carrie to me when Miss Eleanor stated, "Okay, next is Jeanie. I know she's got some interesting pictures for us to see." She grew quiet like she was whispering a secret, only we could all hear, "Go ahead now, Jeanie, and you'll do fine."

I took one look around the circle and then glanced back to Miss Eleanor. "Miss Eleanor? I don't want to do this. My pictures are dumb and I don't feel so good. Could you just please go on? Could you please?"

She might have let me off the hook until Mark blurted out, "If I had to do it you should too." Then the others in the circle added their chorus of good natured yeahs. Even Carrie.

"But . . . but Miss Eleanor?" I said. I was one inch away from pleading.

"Oh, Jean," twelve-year-old Jim stated, "just do it and get it over with."

Miss Eleanor leaned forward in her chair and nodded her head.

"Seems like your friends want to hear what you have to say. You wouldn't want to let them down, would you?"

I didn't know what else to do. "All right," I sighed, giving Jim a nasty look. "All right, but I don't want to do it."

I opened my Bible and pulled out my snapshots. I looked around the circle slowly, taking in each face, each expression before I had the courage to begin.

"Well . . . I guess I'll start with . . . with my cat Popcorn."

Everyone laughed, including Miss Eleanor, until I flashed the picture of Popcorn in the snow for them to see. Then a few girls went, "Ah, she's cute!" Carrie turned her head sideways and said, "Let me see! Let me see! Let me see!" until I passed the photo into her eager hands.

"Popcorn's four years old and I love him a lot. He's mine. I'm the only one he comes to."

"Go on, go on," Mark insisted. "I hate cats. Back to your family."

"But Popcorn *is* my family," I replied seriously. "All right, let's see. Most of you know I'm the youngest in the family—"

"The baby," Jim laughed.

I ignored him and repeated, "I'm the *youngest* in my family and the brother right above me is Bernie. He's almost three years older than me and he likes to build things. People say we look alike. Bernie has sandy hair. Blue eyes. He's a freshman at the high school. Here he is working on his bike." I held the picture for them to examine, then continued, "He can tell the funniest jokes. I mean really funny. He's got a big heart and I like having him for my brother . . . well, most of the time. Especially when we're not fussing."

I returned the picture to my lap. Next in line was Christine. She was seventeen, and one and a half years away from graduation. She had spent all her junior high years in different hospitals with a disease that wouldn't let go. I remember the happiness of finally having her home as my big sister again, even though she had to spend another whole year in bed. Tutors from school were in and out of our house all the time. Dr. Bradford, too. That was a couple years ago, and she was now back on the track in her schooling.

"Here's Tina," I said and raised her picture, "my one and only sister. She's what you call mature for her age. She helps me with my homework. We sometimes listen to the radio or watch T.V. together. She got her license a few months ago. She's at school a lot and I . . . I don't see her as much. Here she is in one of her school pictures. Her hair's shorter now and it looks darker brown than what it shows here. Anyway, it's the only recent one I could find."

When the last of the children had looked at Christine's photograph I went on to find Peter's. I stared a long time at his face in the picture. Someone had snapped the camera while Peter sat in the overstuffed living room chair and held me in his lap. I think he was feeding me an orange slice. Maybe it was a piece of apple. I was two years old then.

Peter was about the gentlest brother in the world. I was always so proud of him. He had a million friends and he was in lots of activities. Band was his favorite. I never heard a single soul in my whole life say anything unkind about Peter. People at church. Or neighbors. Or teachers who had us both as students. I guess it was because he put his whole heart into everything he tried. He was smart also, but he never came off as conceited or anything like that. People liked to be around him. I knew I did. I studied his face in the picture and felt my lower lip quiver. I missed him so much. Dad felt Peter was siding with Mother when they got to arguing about the divorce, so he kicked him out late last summer. How I missed him.

"I think you all know Peter," I said to my circle of friends, "because he works with the senior highs upstairs. I'm not sure, but I think he's nineteen or twenty. Peter's supposed to be a junior in Bible college but he had to sit this year out to earn some money. He'll go back. I know he will. He's wanting to be a minister or social worker or something like that. I don't get to see him as much since he got an apartment, but I'd sure like to. My brother Peter is special, kind of like a hero to me. I've always looked up to him. I think I always will. By the way, this picture's nine or ten years old!"

I sucked in a deep breath. There was only one photograph left in my hand. It was an old picture of my parents taken before I was born. If I felt choked up when I looked at Peter's face a moment ago, I was *really* choked up when I studied the expressions on my parents' faces. They were sitting beside each other at the end of the supper table and they were laughing. Actually laughing! I couldn't even remember the last time I'd seen them laugh together or sit so close.

It might have been cold in the seventh grade classroom, but I was getting hotter by the second. "Well . . . I don't know exactly what to say about my mother. She taught Bible school here last summer and she helps out in the church office now and then. She just got another job to help . . . to help . . . just to help, that's all." How could I admit it was because Father had cut off all money to her except twenty dollars a week? Even I knew that didn't go far enough to feed five people and take care of the other expenses like my medicine, or Tina's, or Mom's.

I continued, "Nobody can cook like my mother. She's the best, and I'm pretty close to her." That was the truth, too, especially since the November episode with my father in the car. I never told a soul about that day on the freeway, and neither had Father for all I knew, but since then I gravitated to my mother like I never had before.

"Here's the picture," I stated. "I'm done."

In my eagerness to finish I shuffled my photographs together and threw them in my Bible.

"Look, she's blushing!" Jim said.

"I am not," I snapped. "It's just warm in here."

"Jeanie," Miss Eleanor quickly interjected, motioning for Jim to keep quiet. "Do you have some final things to say? About the bond of love in your family? And you didn't mention a thing about your father."

I felt as though the room temperature must have been at least a hundred degrees. My upper lip was sweating and I nervously wiped it dry. Every second felt like an hour.

Miss Eleanor waited. All the kids stared at me.

I panicked. I simply panicked under the pressure and the made-up lies came tumbling out. "You'd . . . you'd all like my dad if you knew him. He works midnights and he needs his rest or he'd be here in church right now. He . . . he loves the Lord with all his heart and he . . . he reads from the Bible when we sit down together to eat supper. When I get hurt, like hit my knee or cut my elbow or fall, he prays with me and I feel better. He's like that with Bernie, but not so much with Christine because she's older and can pray for herself.

"Sometimes Dad will race me and Bernie on our bikes. He's always doing things like that. Always. He's about the best dad you could ever want. He tucks me in very night before he leaves for work. He's so kind. He always cares. Peter follows in his footsteps, so to speak. That's why I like Peter so much.

"And you want to know about love?" I couldn't stop. I was building up momentum. My eyes got watery red and I kept going despite my voice that cracked from strain. "My dad . . . my dad loves us so much I don't even know what I'd do without him. I don't. I don't think I could live. Really."

Now the tears were flowing and I fixed my eyes on the ceiling. I couldn't stand to look anyone in the face. "Both my parents tell us kids every single day they love us . . . and they mean it, too. Not all kids are lucky enough to have parents like mine. They might not have a big fancy house for us or a fancy new car or give us tons of fancy clothes, but the one thing they have to hold us together is their love. Real love, not that phony stuff the world offers. You know, to have parents who constantly love you is the greatest thing in the world. It makes all the difference. Absolutely all the difference. *Believe me. I know.*"

I bowed my head and let the tears roll down my cheeks. They splashed like drops of bitter rain onto my Bible. I made no attempt to whisk them away. I tried to move, but couldn't. Even the room was perfectly still except for one sound. While I silently cried I could hear Carrie moving in her seat, sniffling next to me. Was she crying too? Had I been that convincing for them? Couldn't they see right through me? Couldn't they see the lies? My guilt? That I was a pitiful slave to shame?

"Well, class, I hardly know what to say," Miss Eleanor spoke softly. "Thank you, Jeanie, thank you so much for that *beautiful* explanation of the importance of love in family life. Children, I've never heard or seen it put in better terms for us all to understand. It's obvious Jeanie knows this kind of love and appreciates what she has. I know her parents would be so proud of her right now."

I continued to weep, only harder. Was my teacher making me out to be some type of martyr? A model child in a model family? What have I done? What have I created? I could hardly stand it. I wanted to run out of the room and never come back. Never.

Miss Eleanor thumbed through her Bible to find First Corinthians. She spoke again, "It fits so well with one of our memory verses. Listen as I read, 'And if one member suffers, all the members suffer with it; if one member is honored, all the members rejoice with it.'

"The kind of Christian body Paul is talking about is the kind that unites. If one member hurts, they all hurt. If one's happy, they're all happy. And if families stick together, it's with this kind of love Jeanie has mentioned. Hear me, children: that's what families are all about! That's what the family of God is all about!

"Thank you again, honey," the teacher said and offered a clean folded tissue to me. "Jesus will bless you."

I barely heard Miss Eleanor. The lies I told spoke louder to me than all her words. *"Oh, God,"* I prayed inside, *"forgive me. Please forgive me."*

4

Visions

"NO, FATHER," I said and squinted my eyes against the harsh morning light. "I don't think I want to go today."

He reached for the kitchen counter to maintain his balance. "What do you mean?" he slurred. "What d'you mean telling me *you don't want to go?* It's that damn attorney and your mother, isn't it? Telling you not to go? Isn't it? *Isn't it?*"

"It's Saturday morning," I returned. "I . . . I don't feel so good. Can't Mom take me to get boots later on?"

"You're comin' with me if I have to tie you up and throw you in the trunk of the car! Now go on and get dressed!" he shouted and thrust a sharp pointed finger my way. Red veins raised on his angry face.

I gulped hard and my heart was racing. "Please God," I frantically prayed. "Please get Bernie or Christine to wake up."

"Didn't you hear me? I said *move it!*" I hated it since he began talking to us the past months in that swaggering tone of voice. It always meant trouble.

"But . . . but Mom can take me when she gets home from work. Besides, winter's almost over. It's the end of February. I've made it this far without boots. I . . . I guess I don't need them much now."

Father's arms gesticulated wildly. "No! The courts think I'm an unfit father. That's what they think, you know. Your mother's got everyone believing I do wrong all the time. That hearing last week was a *mockery*. You hear me? A *mockery*. So I'm gonna show them all. You need boots, you're gonna get boots! You're comin' with me!"

I glanced at the kitchen clock. "But the stores. They aren't even open yet. Won't be for another hour or two. Can't *she* take me? Please?"

"Aww, she's got the whole lot of you brainwashed. Brainwashed! That's what it is. Makin' you fear your own daddy."

Tears of helplessness and panic slid over my cheeks. Why was I only twelve years old? Why could I not stand my own ground? Resist him? Why was I caught in the middle again? Why?

I flashed back to that traumatic November day in the rain. I would never go through that again in the car with him. Never. He could beat me to a bloody pulp, knock me unconscious, but I wasn't ever going back inside that car with him alone. Never. Never again.

"No," I whispered and shook my young head back and forth. "I . . . I can't go today."

"Why you damn little—" He started toward me, lost his balance, and fell. If I had any doubts about his condition before, they were now confirmed: it was Saturday morning and Father was drunk. In fact, I think he was more intoxicated than I'd ever seen him.

He lay on the cold kitchen tile in a stupor, cursing God, the Democrats, the chilly floor, me, and my mother. *Especially my mother.* The more he raved the more panicked I became. "You've done it now," I thought to myself. "Now there'll be trouble to deal with all weekend and it's your own fault."

Dazed, my father clutched at a dining room chair to pull himself up. He was infuriated! Now was my chance. In a flash I darted for Christine's room. I flew down the corridor, around the sharp corner, and through her doorway. Quickly I turned the metal lock on the knob behind me.

"Tina! Tina! Wake up!" I screamed and shook her fiercely. "It's Dad. He's been drinking. I'm scared, Tina. Really scared. Hide me. Get me out of here. *Do something!*"

Christine's brunette curls flopped to the right side of her face when I pulled her forward. "What is it this time?" She threw back the covers and brushed aside the mass of hair.

"He wants me to go away with him. Just him and me. All alone. Something over boots. I'm scared, Tina. He's really upset."

A violent pounding of fists vibrated the wooden door. "Open this door!" Father exclaimed. "I'm going to *kill* you when I get my hands on you, you little—"

Like clockwork, Christine sprang up and reached for the phone while I ran to the bedroom window and checked the distance to ground. Slippers. I didn't have any slippers. Just my bare feet. Snowdrifts around the window were a good two feet high. How could I get the storm window out in time anyway? No screwdriver to unfasten the locks. *Dear God, help me.* The closet. Maybe I could hide there. Or under the bed. No, he'd check.

"Hello, Mother?" Christine shouted over the deafening knocks. "It's Dad. Jean? She's with me. Better get Peter. He's got a knife or screwdriver or something out there. He's taking the pins out of the door now, trying to get at her. Better forget Peter. Get the police."

There was a long pause then Tina continued, "Who, Bernie? I think I hear him up. Right. He's trying to talk Dad away from the door. Mother, it's crazy! Hurry!"

Christine slammed down the telephone and we both listened intently to the dialogue in the outer hallway. The way my heart pounded through my chest, it was amazing I could hear anything.

"Let them alone, Dad," Bernie urged. "Come on. Let them alone. Please? Please just go sit down and cool off."

"Oh?" Father hollered back sarcastically "Another country heard from? No fifteen-year-old kid of mine is telling me what to do. Now get the hell out of here while you can still walk!"

The scratching of metal against metal on the other side of the door subsided long enough to offer the sound of flesh upon flesh. Bernie cried out in sharp pain. "There now," Dad said, "that ought to teach you who's running this show!"

"Show?" I uttered to Christine and paced nervously back and forth. "Show? God, I'm scared! Tina, I'm so scared! What's he gonna do to me?"

"You're shaking," she comforted. "We'll make it. Don't worry. We'll make it through this one. Try to calm down."

"Open this!" came the command again. Father was jerking the doorknob angrily. "Damn you! Do it *now* or you'll regret the day you were born!"

"I do already!" I sobbed to Tina and wiped my flannel sleeve against my wet face. "Do I ever!"

Suddenly there was silence. No pounding. No scraping of his knife against the pins or doorknob. Just silence. Pure silence.

"Think he's fainted?" I whispered. "Think he's still out there? Maybe he'll crash through the window or something like that."

"Shh!" Christine answered and touched her ear against the door to listen.

More unbearable silence.

"Didn't I tell you to get lost?" Father exploded from his side of the divider.

"Bernie," I concluded for Christine. "Bernie's back."

"Please, Dad. Listen to me. Just leave them alone, okay?" Bernie was cautious enough not to raise his voice when Dad was drinking. He was such a good brother in times of stress.

"Seems it's time for a little power!" Father yelled. I closed my eyes tight. I knew what that meant.

Bernie tried hard to be brave. It was a full minute before the house was filled with his cries—youthful cries I'd never heard the likes of before, and could never forget.

"Jeanie? Jeanie?" Christine said and touched my shoulder. I recoiled in fear. "Jean. I'm going to open this door. And when I do, I want you to run straight ahead. Tear out as fast as you can. Do you hear me? Run for the front door. Head over to Webbers'. They'll take you in. You got to run fast, all right?"

"But Bernie," I wept, "and you!"

"Run as fast as your legs can travel, hear? We'll handle things at this end. Head for Webbers'. *Don't stop until you're there!*"

"Webbers'," I babbled. "Webbers'. Don't stop. Run fast."

"Go!" Christine shouted, pulling open the door.

I was not prepared for the partially blocked passageway that led to the front exit. Pinned there, on the floor beneath my father's heavy knees, was Bernie's chest. Although my father's back was toward me, I could tell by his swinging arms that the punishment for my brother's crime of love continued.

"Run, Jeanie! Run!" Bernie screamed, lifting his head from the carpet. I stopped cold when I saw the terrible expression on my brother's face. How many blows had he taken in my place? How many? And how could he lie there willingly, taking such punishment? Punishment meant for me.

"For God's sake get out of here!" Christine yelled.

"Bernie, I'm . . . I'm so sorry. I'm so, so sorry," I wailed and shot past them before Father could grasp what was happening. "Forgive me, Bernie! Dear Jesus, forgive me!"

I found it odd that I should think of cold snow on my feet at a time when I was running for my life. I mean, so long as I made it out alive, why care about cakes of ice between my toes? And why think now of these tattered pajamas? The Webbers knew I would have had the good sense to wear a nicer pair if I'd anticipated an early morning stroll through the neighborhood. Today? Today I didn't care about shame or pajamas or bare feet. I just wanted to live. I just wanted my brother and sister safe.

The echoes of my frozen fists urgently pounding on their aluminum storm door could have awakened everyone on the street. Still, why would they not answer? "Come on," I said anxiously. "Please come on!"

I knocked more fiercely and shifted from one cold foot to another. When I reached down to brush aside a piece of road salt that had punctured one bleeding toe, I heard the sweet sound of air suction as Mr. Webber opened the inside door. He was just waking up.

"For goodness' sake!" he exclaimed and jerked me into his living room. "It's freezing outside. Here, let me get you a blanket and some towels for your feet."

He left me for a moment and hollered up the stairwell to his wife. "Honey, do you think you can come down here? I think there's trouble over at Jeanie's house."

By the time Mrs. Webber rushed down the stairs I was shaking uncontrollably. Partly from the bitter air outside. Mostly from the crushing fear within.

"Your father?" she sighed.

I nodded yes. Without a word Mrs. Webber guided me over to the couch and grabbed for the blanket that her husband offered. I was panicked beyond the point of feeling warmth of any kind, from her strong arms or from the wool comforter.

"Pretty bad?" she asked.

"Yes," I sobbed. "Yes, it's my father. Yes. He's . . . he's been drinking. He wanted me to go away with him, but I was afraid. Over some boots. I went in to wake up Christine. By then Bernie was up and tried to calm him down. When I left Dad was hitting on him pretty hard. Bernie needs help and it's all my fault."

"Your mother not home?" one of them asked.

"She . . . she works on Saturdays. Figured we'd be safe if we were together at home. But Bernie—somebody's got to help Bernie."

Mr. Webber paced the floor. "This can't go on. You kids shouldn't have to live like this." He reached for a shirt from around the corner and proceeded to put it on.

"Christine just now called Mother at work," I spoke. "Mom was supposed to call Peter or the police or her lawyer. It . . . it was awful."

"Didn't your father throw Peter out?" asked Mrs. Webber.

"No one's supposed to know it, but yeah," I answered and pulled the blanket closer. "About seven or eight months ago. Dad said Peter was always siding with my mother over the divorce stuff. I wish it was done with. From week to week it gets worse. More tension. More things said or done in spite. Sometimes I wake up and wonder what is real anymore. Am I home now, asleep? Is this a nightmare? Will I ever wake up?"

"How long has it been going on?" Mrs. Webber asked.

"What? Stuff like today?"

I waited. I couldn't tell if she nodded yes or no. My teeth were chattering from the cold, but I forced the answer. "It's been a year and a half since Mother filed. Things were pretty bad then but nothing like now. Why do they have to keep going at it? Why can't they just get it over with? Why does my father have to fight it and stay? Nothing makes sense!"

"It looks like your brother is there now," Mr. Webber announced, pulling open the picture window curtain so I could see. I did not look. "Isn't that Peter's silver car in the driveway?"

"I think I'm getting sick," I announced and jumped up.

"Quickly! In here!" Mrs. Webber said and rushed me to the bathroom toilet. I went through the motions of throwing up, but no food came. Only stomach juices. I hadn't had breakfast yet.

"Your dad's out on the sidewalk with Peter," called Mr. Webber from the living room. "I can't tell what happened exactly, but your brother's sure taking a beating. This has to stop. *I'm going over.*"

I could hear Mr. Webber search through the closet for his overcoat. "Honey," he yelled to his wife, "you better call the authorities just in case they haven't been notified. No telling what he's done to the other two inside."

Mrs. Webber left my side for the phone. Mr. Webber darted out the front door. I stood alone, trembling and in tears, heaving over the toilet.

Days may pass. Visions do not. There were visions when I returned home Saturday morning that I would never forget. *Never.* It was all my fault. I was sure of it. It was I my father wanted, not any of them. My sister and brothers must have hated me for what I'd done. Each had endured tremendous physical pain only because I'd said no to Father. How could they stand me? How could they bear to look at me again? Could they ever forget? Could they ever forgive?

Yes, there were permanently etched visions connected with that day, all right. To my left stood Peter, holding his head, telling the policemen no, he wouldn't press charges even though he was of legal age. He knew better when he looked into his younger brother's and sisters' eyes that we would pay a hundred times over for his slight moment of retaliation.

There were visions of Christine's pure and white face. How she could smile was beyond me. Especially since she, too, had withstood the grasps of a rough, unloving hand that morning. She had certainly seen better days in her seventeen years.

And there were visions of Bernie. How could I forget his cleansed, slightly flushed face? Only an hour before it was a horrible image of pain. No screams came from his lips now. No tears from his eyes. He stood strong and tall as though nothing unusual had taken place in our badly broken inner circle.

There were other visions, too, of myself and Father. I was still in my pajamas and scared to death. I was petrified! How could life go on for all of us under the same roof after today? I wanted to cry out. Hide. Get sick all over again. What was happening here? And why was my father smiling? I had learned never to trust his smile. Over the past years and months I had associated his smile with something sinister. It meant he was up to something. Something not good. Something that would hurt me deeply.

"There's no problem here," father matter-of-factly reported to the two officers dressed in gray and black uniforms. How I wish he didn't have that ability to control his anger in front of strangers! Even before he drank he could put on a good display outside the home or when company came. He was putting on his best performance right this minute, and there wasn't a thing any of us could do to stop it. The longer I stood there, the more nauseated I grew from his hospitable conversation. I gritted my teeth at hearing what a God-fearing man he was. A churchgoer. A provider for his small fold.

"So you see," he continued, "Peter was trespassing, and I let him have it. He'd been warned to stay away. But the others?" Father stopped and graciously pointed to Christine, Bernie, and me. "My kids worry an awful lot, you know what I mean?"

At that moment I knew we had lost again. I knew that the very nice policemen would write up their very nice reports and be on their very nice way in their very nice car. But me? I would be left behind to live with escalating fear and nausea and hate. I would sit through days and even weeks of unbearable panic, waiting for my father to repay me. He had become like that over the months of court hearings and growing embitterments. He never forgot.

In hopeless resignation, we children listened to Father as he offered his shallow, made-up excuses and apologies to the policemen for *the little disturbance*. His words and expressions of concern sickened me, and I felt the crescendo of hate swell. Hate like I'd never had. Pure hate. I hated *him* and I hated the fact that we victims were forever caught in his dreadful web, unable to do anything but make matters worse for ourselves. What was the point of arguing? Of begging to differ? Of agitating my father even more? Police or no police, I knew we could never win with Father. At best we might survive, but we could never, never win.

I gazed into the tortured faces of Peter, Bernie, and Tina as they glanced back at me, communicating their wordless decision that we should shoulder and consolidate our burdens. Then, quite unexpectedly and in tenderness, Peter secretly winked at me as if to say, "Hang on, Jeanie. This humiliation will pass. Trust me. Just hang on. We're all in this with you."

How well I knew the struggles of my childhood were always faced alone. I could only guess the same was true for my brothers and sisters. Today, though, became one rare moment in time when we children stood side by side, united in our awkward little band. We had mysteriously pulled together, unlike before, to survive one more day. God only knows how with the mounting record of scars inside. But we would survive this day. Somehow. Together.

5

The Label

COME ON IN, Jeanie. Have a seat. I'm Dr. Willis and I'm the counselor who's been assigned to work with you.

No one told me you were a woman doctor.

Does that bother you?

No, I don't think so. I just never expected a woman, that's all.

Have a seat. Either one is fine. Make yourself comfortable.

I think this one is softer. Yeah, definitely. I'll sit here.

Jeanie, try to relax. We're going to talk awhile, okay?

I guess so.

Jeanie, do you know why your family physician referred you to the Mental Health Center? Dr. Bradford's his name, isn't it?

Uh-huh.

Do you know why you're here?

I'm crazy?

Do you think you're crazy?

I don't know any more. I must be if I'm here. You going to lock me up or something?

Lock you up?

Yeah, lock me up. Crazy people should be locked up.

Didn't anyone explain this to you?

No. No one.

We have no intention of locking you up. All we're going to do is talk. Talk, that's all.

Well, last week when I went back to Dr. Bradford, he called in my mother and said he thought he'd helped all he could. Then he wrote down the center's number and told my mother someone here could help. I figured I must be pretty bad if Dr. Bradford had to wash his hands of me. I must be crazy.

You sound like Dr. Bradford's deserted you.

All I know is what I saw. All I know is that I must be pretty bad off. I ask you, Dr. Willis, how would you like to be called crazy? Or labeled crazy? It's no fun. No fun at all. A label like that sticks.

Who said you were crazy, Jeanie?

Nobody used those exact words. I heard my parents arguing about it. About whose fault it was. My father said all I needed was backbone. That Mother was smothering me too much. That if I didn't worry I wouldn't be sick to my stomach. That I was a real weakling. That something's wrong with me that I'm not tougher.

And how did your mother respond?

I don't know. I went to my room and cried. She probably thinks the same. She thinks if I'm not around to see or hear them, I'm out of it. Out of the struggle, I mean. She doesn't understand how everything's tearing me up. Sometimes I think she's only concerned with my dad and she doesn't even know I exist. Does anyone know I exist? Really exist? I feel like I only get in the way. Like I'd do everybody a great big favor if I dropped over dead. Do you think they would notice me then? Probably not. Probably say I was plain crazy and go on fighting without me.

There's that word crazy *again, Jeanie. Do you honestly think you're crazy?*

Don't know, I told you.

If you had to think up . . . oh . . . several good reasons to prove you were . . . were crazy, what would they be?

Well, everybody tells me how I used to cry as a baby and throw my bottle for all it was worth. Maybe I started out crazy, you think? I hated to go to school. Cried just about every single day that first year. And I used to wet the bed a lot. Does a normal kid do that? Huh? I was the only one of us kids to keep it up so long. And another thing, once at school last year some kids and I were teasing about pulling the fire alarm and I did it. I walked right over to that red box and I pulled it. It sounds pretty crazy to me now. Would a normal kid pull a stunt like that? No, just someone crazy.

Anything else? Anything else that makes you think you're crazy?

All right, I'll tell you. I hate it in the car. Always have. I mean I really, really, really, *really* hate it there. My parents leave me in the car when they go places, and it seems like the stupid thing's breaking down every other week. I hate it there. A normal kid should be able to handle sitting there, but I can't.

What do you do that's so different?

I panic. I used to cry. Now I just sit there and get sick to my stomach. I hate it there. A normal kid wouldn't. A regular kid would take it okay.

So here are your reasons: you cried as a baby, you wet the bed, you pulled a school prank, and you hate it in the car. That doesn't sound crazy to me.

No? Well, try this one. I feel like I want to cry all the time. I mean cry and cry and cry and never stop. No matter where I am, no matter what I'm doing, I just want to cry.

Do you? Do you cry all the time?

No, just in bed at night by myself. Or sometimes when I get up and get ready for school I feel real depressed. I cry just when I'm alone. But I want to cry all the time, Dr. Willis. I want to. That's not normal, is it? My friends at school never talk about crying. They can handle things. Something must be wrong with me. If I was tougher, if I wasn't such a weakling, I could handle everything better. I feel ashamed.

Ashamed of what?

I'm ashamed I'm not stronger.

How old are you?

I'm twelve.

Twelve is mighty young to be tough like you say you want to be.

Well, I don't see my brothers or sister falling apart. They're tough. They can take it.

Tell me about them.

Peter's the oldest. About twenty or so I'd say. He's been off to college the last couple years and he's got an apartment across town now because my dad kicked him out.

So Peter's not really been exposed to the action at home all that much? He's been away for a few years? And he's nine or ten years older than you?

Yes, I guess so. Yes to all your questions.

Tell me about your sister.

She's at school a lot. She was sick for a long, long time, but I think she's coming along better now.

So she's not always at home either?

I . . . I guess not. She's taking a lot of classes so she can graduate maybe by the end of this summer. And she's looking for a part-time job. She told me she'd take anything she could find. She'd like to get her own place to stay.

And your other brother?

Bernie? He's got a paper route and he's in some clubs at the high school. He's got a few buddies in the neighborhood or school that he hangs around with.

Is he home in the evenings?

Well . . . no . . . I guess I don't see him much there at all.

But you? You're there?

Nowhere else to be.

And your parents? Are they home a lot?

Pretty much.

And you're there with them?

Usually.

Alone?

Usually.

Doesn't it make sense you'd be more affected?

But if I was just stronger I could—

I'm not talking about strength. I'm talking about you being the most likely one to be affected simply because you're there more. Sounds to me like your brothers and sister can get out and do other things to occupy their time. But you? How's a twelve-year-old girl supposed to get around? It looks to me like you're kind of a sitting duck.

But I should still be able to take it. At church they're always telling us all we need is God. We can be tough and handle things because we've got God and He's all we need. Nothing else. Nobody else.

Jeanie, let me ask you something. Why are you so hard on yourself?

Hard on myself?

Hard on yourself. Why do you push and demand so much?

I don't know. I guess because I don't want to be weak. I don't want to be a big baby all my life. I feel like everyone at home always makes fun of me and I hate it when they call me a baby. I just hate it. So that's why I've got to be tough. To prove to everybody I'm not a weakling.

Do you think your school or church friends would do better if we put them in your place with your home and parents?

Yep. They can take that kind of stuff.

But how do you know?

I know, that's all. They're stronger.

But they haven't been in your shoes.

So?

So maybe they'd be in worse shape. Maybe they'd be falling apart right now. Maybe they'd have run away. Maybe they'd have done something really drastic.

Well, they look pretty strong to me.

Do you ever talk with your school friends about your problems at home?

Only with one of them. John. He's had it pretty rough. He lives close to me and he's smart. Real smart. We talk a lot. I think he's my best friend.

Tell me about your hobbies. What kind of things do you like to do besides get together with John?

I like to draw, that's a fact. And I read a lot. I own a mess of books. But writing's what I like to do best. Stories. Maybe one day I'll write a book.

Are you working on a story right now?

Kind of. When I can get settled down enough to think clear.

Tell me about the story. The one you're working on now.

Why would you want to hear about that?

I just do. I'd like to hear about what interests you.

I don't see why.

To get to know you, and I like stories. Tell me yours, please?

Okay, but I think this is a waste of time. First, the story's involved. I mean really involved. It's about a submarine. A special sub that's a world first. It's luxurious. Never been one like it ever because it can hold hundreds and hundreds, and it can go anywhere in water. Anywhere. Even under lakes and oceans that are frozen solid on top. It just rolls along. Like I said, it's one of a kind.

It's going to go around the world. All around in one trip, I mean, without stopping. All sorts of important people are on board for its very first voyage. A senator. Business people. Engineers. Some athletes. Even a woman doctor, now that I think of it. But there's this one character who's pretty bad. Crawford's his name. He's filthy rich and always trying to impress people with his money. He's there and his family's there because he donated a million dollars to the project. He wants it named after him. Anyway, he's all flash and he doesn't care much about his kids. He gives them everything but love. Absolutely everything.

Go on. Go on. I'm listening.

Well, the submarine's up around the North Pole by now. It's way under hundreds of feet of ice and miles in. Suddenly there's this power shortage. Zap! Everyone's panicked. They discover they're so far below the ice that their communication systems are useless. There is enough reserve power to control lights and ventilation, but that's about it. It turns out there's a tiny little broken part in the circuit system that's holding everything up. It fits inside this miniature computer. It's kinda hard to explain.

I see. Go on, Jeanie. Don't stop.

This is silly, Dr. Willis. Why am I telling you this story?

Go ahead. It's interesting. Really, I want to listen.

Okay. Well, this guy Crawford I told you about is having trouble with his heart. He's rushed off to their little hospital clinic and the lady doctor checks him over. He's only one step away from a heart attack. Oh—I forgot to tell you—he's got a pacemaker inside. Inside here.

It seems there's this little metal piece in his pacemaker that they could use in the submarine computer to fix it. Somehow Crawford overhears the nurse, doctor, and one of the scientists who designed the engine talking in the next room. Everyone on board will die within twenty-four hours if they don't get that piece, but the doctor's holding out to save Crawford. She says it's her duty. That she couldn't justify taking his life, and that's what it would mean to remove the pacemaker.

Crawford knows he's not supposed to move, but he decides this is the one chance to make up for all the mistakes in his life. He knows nobody likes him. His kids hate him, but they haven't figured out why. Now's his time. He manages to get up, sneak out the side door slowly and with a lot of chest pain, and forces himself up the metal flight of stairs. Higher. Higher. Higher. On purpose.

The strain is too much and he knows it. He gasps out loud. The doctor goes running through the hospital room and outside the door. She flies up the steps, but it's too late. Crawford dies right there in her arms. Now she can remove the pacemaker and everybody's saved. That's it. That's the story. He dies a hero.

How fascinating! Very, very clever, too. You ought to send it out to Hollywood.

You think?

It's as clever as anything I've seen on television.

You really think so? Most of the time I just rip up the stories when I'm done. Pitch them.

This is one you ought to save. Are all the things you write this action-packed?

No, usually they're about things inside of people. Feelings kinds of things. Most of them are sad, though. I guess I'd say all of them are sad in one way or another.

Let's change the topic a minute, Jeanie. It says here in your folder that you complain of a stomach ache a lot. Could you fill me in?

What all do you have there in that folder?

Not much. Just some general facts your mother gave us.

When was she in?

She came in long enough to fill out a form we require. I met her briefly yesterday.

Oh.

How about your stomach?

Sometimes I can't hold my food down. Not a lot of the time, but when I get upset, real upset, it all comes up.

How often?

I don't know. That all depends. If it's a calm week I can manage pretty well. But my stomach feels sore a lot of the time, whether I throw up or not.

Jeanie, I know your parents are divorcing. How do you feel about that?

Honestly?

Honestly.

Is what I say in here just between you and me, Doctor? No one else?

If you want it that way, sure.

How do I feel? How do I really feel? I feel like it'll never end. It's been well over a year—almost two—since Mother filed in the first place. All that time living under the same roof! Will it ever be done with? They get a hearing date scheduled and then something always happens. Someone can't show . . . the judge is called out of town . . . the attorneys think they have a special settlement so they cancel the meeting only to find out one or the other doesn't agree. And my dad—don't ask me why—is fighting this all the way. And my mom? Sometimes she tells us kids she's doing it all for us. And then sometimes she talks about getting back with my dad. Reconciliation is the word, I think. Now that really scares me! How can she forget how awful it gets? I don't. I can never forget.

Jeanie, what do you think you want? What would make you happy in all this at home? What would really satisfy you?

I guess I want my father out! There isn't anything I can think of that I like about him. Not one thing. He can't do anything or say anything to ever win me back. Not ever. It's kind of like a hot iron, Doctor. You don't have to keep rubbing it over a spot on a shirt a million times to burn it. No, all you got to do is hold it there once, long enough, and it'll sear right through. Well, I've been seared through. No more of him. No more. No more, Doctor.

You want to hear something? You want to hear what my dad did last week? Well, Bernie and me have this little go-cart. It's just something we always drag out in spring. It's got an old lawn mower engine on it and I admit it doesn't work so hot, but it's ours. Took a long time to save up for it. Bernie had the motor torn apart on the basement floor because it needed a gasket so it wouldn't leak so much oil. I swear to you we had the engine parts over in a corner out of the way. Well, Saturday night my dad got mad. I think he'd been drinking. He yanked up the parts, took them outside, and smashed them down on the gravel driveway! Bolts, screws, the works! He demolished it! I cried the entire night. I tell you, watching him smash it up right in front of me really hurt. My dad hates me and I hate him. That seems to sum it up real good.

You ask me what I want? I want him O-U-T! I want him *out!* And I want my mother to forget him. To get the hell away from him and take me with her. I don't ever want to see my father again. He's no father. No father at all. I want to get as far away from him as possible and forget everything.

Jeanie, how long's this tension between your parents been going on?

Have you ever had a toothache, Doctor?

Sure I have.

I mean a real bad one that sends you right up to the ceiling?

Once or twice.

The kind you can never forget?

I suppose so.

If I had a toothache like that right now and you asked me how long it's been going on, I'd probably say forever.

Forever?

When I hurt it feels like I've always hurt. Like that tooth has throbbed forever and I somehow lose track of time. Maybe it was only yesterday it started hurting, but I'd never think of that. I'd say it hurt a long, long time.

Back to my question, Jeanie. How long has this tension between your parents been going on?

Forever.

I see. I see.

Forever and ever and ever and ever.

But you're not sure?

I can't give you a date if that's what you want. And I can't remember when it all started, but it seems like forever. I can't remember a time of real happiness for all of us. Sure not for me.

Who in your family can you turn to? Your grandparents? A particular brother or sister?

Three of my grandparents were dead before I was born. I only knew my one grandmother, and she died when I was five. And like I say about my brothers and sister—they're usually off doing whatever they do. I turn to Christine sometimes. Not a whole lot, but sometimes.

Is there a particular teacher at school you feel close to?

Maybe my English teacher, but she quit because she's going to have a baby. The school year will be over with in two or three months anyway.

A neighbor? Someone at a club or church?

No, not really. I used to like this lady named Miss Eleanor at church but no more. I used to break my back to help her out but no more.

Oh? Why's that?

There was only one time I said I didn't want to participate in her class. Only one no after saying yes a hundred times. She egged me on. Even when I said no she wouldn't accept it. I lost my respect for her that day. Now all I do is shrug my shoulders when she asks me things. I figure I'll let her handle the silence any way she wants, but I'm not participating ever again. Besides, because the word has spread and spread about my folks getting a divorce, well, we're looking for a new place to go. Probably some other Baptist church.

Jeanie, I see our time is almost up.

You going to lock me up now?

I don't follow.

Crazy people should be locked up.

No, we're not going to lock you up. There may be things in your world that seem crazy, but you are not crazy.

Sure feels like it in here. Inside me. Trying not to cry. Trying to sleep at night. Trying to hold myself together. Trying not to get sick.

You're attempting to cope with a lot of things. What we'll do is try to sort through what's happening, break everything down so you can understand better. In the meantime, I'm putting you on several kinds of medication. One's for your stomach. Here. You'll take this four times a day. Another's for sleep, and you should take it half an hour before bedtime. This third one's to calm your whole system. I already checked with Dr. Bradford's office. We want you to discontinue the ones he's had you on. Start on these. Only these. Have your mother fill them soon and we'll see how you do.

This is a hopeless situation, you know.

How do you figure?

Unless you can leave here and come home with me, well, I'll still be alone. Mom will still be the same. Dad the same. And me alone. There's not much hope in that. There never has been.

Get the medication filled. How about if we schedule you next Tuesday at this same time?

I suppose so.

Would you like your mother to sit in then?

Why?

Sometimes children your age feel better if one of their parents is present with them.

No, I don't think I'd like that. I don't see how it'd help. She'd probably have a fit if she knew I was telling everything. She wouldn't like that. I don't want her here. You can talk with her alone if you like, but I don't want her here when it's my turn.

Fine. I just thought I'd ask.

Is that it?

One last question: how do you feel?

About coming here? Or feel inside?

Either one.

I don't know if I can handle being labeled a crazy. Sooner or later, you watch, at home or at school, I'll be called crazy, crazy, crazy.

Sometimes people are insensitive. We'll cross that bridge if we ever come to it. It's not always important what other people think of us. What counts is what we think of ourselves. What matters is if Jeanie Campbell thinks Jeanie Campbell is crazy.

You got me there.

What do you mean?

There are times I think I am crazy. Times I think I'm not. Times

I just don't know. Times I just don't care. Times I want to quit. Quit everything.

We'll talk about that next Tuesday, all right?

Yeah. Yeah, if you say so.

See you, Jeanie.

You too.

'Bye for now.

Yeah. 'Bye.

6

Against My Will

I KNEW IN MY heart what had to be done.

I gathered my books and purse and reached for the silver door handle. "Really, it won't hurt me to walk home from here, Mr. Webber," I said. "It's only a little way."

Mr. Webber seemed troubled. "All right, if you're sure you'll be okay."

"I'm sure," came my weak reply.

"Call if you need anything. I'm off the rest of this month. You know, I wanted to take my vacation early this year. April seems cool enough. Beats that summer heat," he said, trying to sound cheerful.

"Yeah," I agreed, closing his car door behind me. "Thanks again you came to pick me up. Like I said, I . . . I didn't want the school to bother Mom at work. Or my dad at home. Mr. Webber, you're a good neighbor. A good one. I'll miss . . ." I knew better than to finish my thought out loud.

"You'll miss what?" he puzzled and stroked his jutting chin.

"Oh, nothin'," I stammered. "Nothin' important."

"Feeling any better now?"

"I'm tired. I'm real, real tired."

He added gently, "And your tummy?"

"I think it's tired too," I sighed and touched my stomach. I walked around the car as I continued, "It . . . it hit in the middle of class. I don't know why, but I just couldn't stop throwing up. Maybe it's the flu. Maybe it's a bad case of the flu. I don't feel so hot. I want to get in bed. Think I'll go now, Mr. Webber. I'll just cut across your lawn here and go home."

"Jeanie, you be careful."

I stopped on his sidewalk and turned to face him. "Be careful?" I questioned as the familiar moisture filled my eyes once again.

"Take care of yourself, I mean."

There was nothing to do but motion good-bye.

Yes, in my heart I knew what had to be done and I knew today was the day. No more waiting for another time. No more postponing. No more secret bartering, "I'll do it if such and such happens," or, "I won't do it if I feel better tomorrow." No more. All my tomorrows had come to naught and I knew this—above and beyond all such times—this was the day.

I eased shut the house door with my left shoulder, deposited my belongings on a counter's edge, and extended my free hands down to meet Popcorn. "Be quiet, kitty," I warned. "We must be quiet." Popcorn responded with a chorus of meows and rubbed his small dark body back and forth against my ankles.

"I said be quiet, boy," I repeated. "Please, just this once?"

With more caution than usual I tiptoed through the kitchen and began the steep upward climb to my second-floor bedroom. "No, Popcorn, no!" I whispered as he maneuvered himself between my feet. One of Popcorn's favorite tricks had always been to weave back and forth through my legs on the way up, but today I did not want our shuffle to be heard by my sleeping father. No doubt he would be mad I was home again and wouldn't believe I was sick. I don't think anyone ever believed me. No, they probably figured I was still faking or was just a spineless weakling. One or the other.

Popcorn dashed ahead of me to the top of the stairs and turned around to watch me come. All I could see was his black face bobbing at me one way, then another, and his silver thread whiskers dancing like a marionette's strings. He wanted to play. He wanted me to shoo him and clap my hands so he could dart impulsively through the upstairs bedrooms. But today was not a day for games; I was much too drained for that.

After the long ascent I pulled off my shoes and set them neatly beside the wooden banister in the hallway. I even took a moment to tuck the untied laces beneath the leather tongue of each shoe as had been my habit for years. Surprised, I stopped and studied my young hands. They were amazingly calm despite the fierce pounding heartbeats that continued to pulse blood and life through my chest against my will. Pounding harder. Harder. Harder. Pounding against my will.

Before I straightened up I reached out and invited Popcorn into my arms. I cuddled him tenderly. "I love you, kitty," I said. "I love you because you are mine. No one else's. You did everything right, Popcorn. Everything. I think you're the only one I'll really miss. And I bet you're the only one who'll miss me. Bet so, Popcorn. Bet so. You just watch. I know I'm right.

"Do you know I love you? I guess I said that. You're the only one I love. The *only* one. You never doubt me and you notice I'm alive. You listen when I talk. You let me be me. Wish you could come with me, boy, but that's okay. I'm kind of used to being alone, and I'm pretty sure someone will take care of you. Think they will do that for me? I hope so, Popcorn. I hope so because I love you."

I kissed his head again and again and brushed my tears from his shiny fur. Then I set him down and made my way through the darkened hallway. There, just around the corner, was Christine's cedar chest. And there, buried inside that red-burned box and forgotten years ago, was precisely what I wanted to complete my task.

Within seconds I was sitting in the center of my bed, legs folded and arms resting on my knees. I knew if I waited too long I might lose my nerve again. For all my thoughts about this hour, for all my hidden plans, I had never come this close before. I had never felt this courageous and certain beyond all doubt that today was the day.

Even though I'd intentionally left the bedroom lamp off, there was enough natural light coming from the nearby window to examine the two items before me. I decided to inspect the three-inch tan envelope first. Holding the little packet close to my face I could just make out the pencil marks scribbled over the closing tab. The numbers were smudged from age, but it appeared the corner notation was 27 cal. short, or perhaps 22 cal. short. I couldn't tell for sure.

"Not now, Popcorn," I groaned as the cat nudged his body into my lap. "Down there, boy. Down there." I coaxed him to his second-favorite resting place, the lower corner of the mattress. "Good boy. You sleep and let me get back to this."

Finally I tore open the paper container and watched the dozen polished bits tumble forth like splashes of crystal rain in a spring shower. Over and out of my hand the fragments bounced until they rested motionless on the crumpled bedding. Their reflecting rays magically invited me to hold, feel, and see for myself. They nearly sparkled in the morning light.

I searched through the fold of the top sheet, produced a tiny metal piece, and studied it closely between my thumb and forefinger. The fairly round, smooth cone at one end showed imperfect scratches etched in the copper head. Minute scratches. It looked like hundreds or more of them. And then, separated only by three distinct ridges and a frail thin ring of silver, was the brass barrel. Inside it, I knew, was the powder. Not just any kind of powder, but *the* powder. *The explosive black powder. The powerful, life-ending powder.*

Hypnotized by the sight of the metallic bit in my one hand, I fingered over the linen with my other, for I realized all too well that a bullet was of no use by itself. My left hand pawed and sifted clumps of wrinkled sheets until it hit its target—the cold, hard steel barrel of a gun. It was the very same gun my father had purchased for our family's protection back in the days when our possible enemy might have come from without.

I pulled the small revolver to my lap for inspection. What an incredible amount of weight for only five or six inches of refashioned nickel ore. Two pearl-white strips of wood or plastic were screwed into the sides of the gun's handle, and each had checked diamond marks carved in deep, graceful crisscross lines. The pattern was beautiful. As I turned the handle around I discovered the imprinting of a long serial number burned into the steel surface. I noticed other engravings on the gun, too. Along the silvery barrel was the manufacturer's name, Smith & Wesson, and just above the blue trigger was stamped a fanciful *W* with a capital *S* woven through it. The distinctive, classic style of the letters showed both strength and frailty, reminding me of a peaceful never-never land so very far away.

The real attraction that morning, however, was the nickel cylinder. Small. Shiny. Very shiny. Reflecting part of my face. The cylinder was movable and it clicked as I turned it. Even with force it wouldn't rotate left. Only right. One click. Two clicks. Three. Around and around it went. I paused to count six blank chambers inside it. Not five or seven holes, but six.

I didn't need to see anything else. I knew what I had to do and that my time had come. Before my thumb thrust the tiny bullet in place, I pressed the empty barrel into my pillow and pulled the trigger to see if the hammer and spring functioned after years of idleness. They did.

Now came the moment of truth. The bullet was in place. I had clicked the cylinder four times to the right until I was sure it was in its correct position. Everything was set. Everything was ready. One finger impulse at the side of either temple and it would all be over. Finished. Done. No more struggles. No more confusion. No more crying or throwing up or humiliation. No more loneliness. No more panic and nightmares. It would be done at last.

I dropped to my knees to offer a final prayer. I waited there an eternity in silence first, my head buried in both palms and pressed against the mattress. I sobbed quietly. This was it. This was my closing act of mercy.

"God," I whispered, "God, are You there? It's me. It's Jeanie. My heart feels like it's pounding right through my chest, so I don't know if I'll be making a lot of sense, but I just wanted to say a few things. God? God, I thought You liked me. There was a time I really thought that. And then a while ago I heard there wasn't anything good in us. I heard it at church and I looked it up for myself and it says it right there in the Bible that there is nothing good that dwells in me. Nothing good. Nothing.

"I haven't been able to get that verse out of my mind. I try but I can't. It just stays there day and night. Over and over. I'm no good. Nothing good in me. It doesn't stop. God, how displeasing mankind must be to You, and how sinful and worthless I must be. How it must turn *Your* stomach just to look at me. I don't mean to disgust You, really I don't. I just don't seem to be doing anything right. Nothing. I can't think of one thing I do right.

"I don't know what's happening to me anymore. The fear will not be stopped. I am afraid at all times of everything. I am afraid to get up. Afraid to sleep. Afraid to be by myself. Afraid with others. Afraid everywhere. Dr. Bradford couldn't help. That counselor hasn't either. There's only one thing I'm not afraid of. It's death. I don't think death could be worse than this.

"I know You want Your people strong and I have failed You. *I have tried and I have tried and I am not strong.* I cannot face another day. I am a coward. Sometimes I think You must have put me here in this family to punish me for being so weak. Or because You don't love me. Did You, God, did You love me ever? Is that how I got here? God, I cannot go on. I am so alone. I feel like I don't matter to anyone and that all I do is get in everybody's way. No one ever talks to me or spends time with me like I'm anything important. So I must not be worth much. Maybe nothing. Maybe I'm not worth a thing. Maybe that explains why I deserve to be miserable.

"God, it's almost time now. I've thought about this day for weeks and weeks. Some people will think it's a cowardly way to go, but do You know how I feel? I feel it's the first time in my life I've ever had courage. The very first time. It's not just this home I want to get away from, but it's this hell inside. I'm dying inside. I'm falling apart inside.

"You know I don't mean to talk back to You, but I was really born against my will. You never came to me and said, 'Jeanie, want to be born?' If You had, and if I could have seen ahead to this life and what it was going to be like, I would have told You flat out *no.* God, there's nothing I found here that's really worthwhile. Life seems like such a waste. It's been a downhill trip all the way. *All the way.* And all the way I watched it go down, down, down, down against my will. It doesn't seem fair, God. It doesn't seem fair that any little kid should wake up and find he's on a one-way trip down and not be able to do anything about it. Someone sends him flying a hundred miles straight down into a brick wall, and he can't do anything. He's helpless. He just sees that wall coming and tries to cover his face with his arms and hands. And in time he smashes dead center into that brick wall against his will. And he bleeds all over the place against his will. And he breathes and he suffers and he hurts—*God, does he hurt*—against his will. It doesn't seem right. God, it doesn't seem fair he gets punished for just being alive. Not when it's all against his will. Every bit of it. That's no life for a kid. That's no life at all. If all he needed was You, why didn't You help him more? Why didn't You help *me* more?

"Well . . . I . . . I just have two final requests and then I won't trouble You anymore here. The first has to do with me and when I die. *Can I come home?* Can I come home and be with You? Do You think You could take all this hurt away or make it so I don't feel anything? Could You make it so I'm not disgusting in Your sight anymore? Could You make me strong?

"The last thing has to do with Popcorn. Could You see that he's taken care of? Could You see that he gets fed and that they don't leave him outside in winter? I know it's spring now and winter's a long way off, but it'll be too cold for him out there and he might run away. Just see he's taken care of. Please, God? See they don't mistreat him.

"I guess that's all. I'm sorry for everything. I wish I could have been better for You. I don't know what else to say so I guess this is it. Amen."

I pulled a rumpled corner of one sheet to my face and swabbed the wetness away. Then I cupped damp strands of hair behind my ears and reached across to a round bedstand for tissues to blow my nose. My legs throbbed from kneeling so long, and instead of rising to sit on the bed by Popcorn, I swung around on my back to rest on the wooden floor. I cocked my hands behind my neck as a kind of headrest. I shut my eyes against the window-framed April sky and sucked in air and thought.

I pictured my family members and how each of them would react to the news. They would be surprised, that was for sure. Who among them would have guessed the seriousness of my despair all along? Not one. Not a single one. Perhaps they would care about me once I was dead, perhaps not. Maybe they would cry and maybe they would write me off as plain crazy.

Was this crazy? Was taking my life crazy? I wondered. Someone who had everything to live for would say yes. Someone who was worn and tired and lonely would say no. I felt the answer was no. In my heart it was no. It would be my choice. It would be my option. I knew what I was doing. I wasn't in some drunken stupor. I wasn't flying around wildly and hallucinating. I knew what I was doing.

I sat up. The bed was still there, Popcorn also, and the metal deposits directly in the center of the white linen. I looked intently at the gun, then down at my hands. For the first time they were trembling. In fact, they were shaking harder than ever before in my twelve years. I watched them in disbelief and felt that familiar, uncontrollable panic spread and spread and spread until I became faint, lightheaded, weak.

"Oh God, help me do this," I anguished and attempted to stretch forth one rigid arm. Paralyzed, I could not so much as lift it off the mattress. "God help me!" I reiterated angrily, straining my muscles a hundred times harder.

An atomic blast on the second floor of the house would not have startled me more than the piercing ring of the telephone. I jerked in alarm so forcefully that Popcorn darted off the corner of the bed in sheer panic and scampered straight out of the room and down the steps lightning fast.

"Wait, boy!" I called out and jumped to my feel impulsively. "Wait! I didn't mean to scare you. I'm sorry, Popcorn!"

By then it was too late. Father, roused by the phone and my voice upstairs, hollered from the doorway below, "What the devil you doing home today?"

A different kind of fear flushed across my face. I glanced down at the bullets and handgun, and reasoned I must hide them and *hide them now!* "Ah . . . ah . . . I got sick at school. They sent me home. You better get the phone!"

I stood breathless, waiting to hear whether Father would come upstairs or grab the telephone by the kitchen.

"Hello?" I heard him say one floor below.

Relief! Killing myself now seemed the farthest thing from my mind. My immediate concern was funneling all twelve bullets back into the tan envelope pouch with nervous awkward fingers and replacing everything back into Christine's storage chest before Father could get off the phone. My hands flashed faster than any magician's, and my legs pumped more swiftly than any athlete's. Down went the lid to the cedar box and I rushed from the corridor as though my life depended on it.

"What's all the noise up here?" Father demanded from three feet away.

I pulled the sheets closer to my pale cheeks. "I . . . I don't feel so good."

"You sure are making a lot of noise. And you're missing too much school. Too much."

"I'll try to go back tomorrow," I uttered and turned my face into the pillow.

"This room's a mess. Get it cleaned up."

"Yes," I said. "I will. After I sleep some. I think I'd like to sleep some now."

"Yeah? Well, keep the noise down," he warned and stepped out of sight. As quickly as he had come, he was gone.

I guess a person who leaves in the middle of a sad movie never knows how it ends, I thought to myself. The gun now put away, I decided to stay for the finale. Besides, I was too tired anymore to fight the performance. Too tired anymore to leave the theatre. Against my will I would stay. I would watch other scenes play out in my life's drama for a while longer—against my will.

"God, please erase this day forever," I cried. "And please give me sleep."

Thoroughly exhausted, I closed my eyes tight and slipped away to quiet dreams.

7

Heaven

I LOOKED STRAIGHT into the heavens and inhaled deeply. In my whole life I had never seen a more beautiful summer sky. Full, rich clouds were everywhere, and they sailed with perfect ease on June winds across their azure backdrop. Large white puffs were overhead. A misshapen elephant, perhaps. A laughing dragon. Two turtles side by side. And smaller, smoky vapor dots were coming in from the west. Yes, I reasoned, heaven must be like this. Heaven must be blue and white and just this peaceful.

I glanced back down to the road and quickly steered my bike left onto Elm Street. Gravel spurted out from the wobbly front rubber tire as I rounded the corner. To regain my balance I quickly tapped the brakes with my feet three times. It worked. I was off again and building speed.

"Hey, Johnny!" I yelled ahead to my best friend. "John, hold up! Wait for me!"

"Jeanie!" the twelve-year-old boy shouted back. He glanced both ways over his shoulders for possible traffic on the deserted road, then made a huge half circle and retraced his journey. "I'm coming!"

Each of us stood up and pedaled hurriedly toward the other until the gaping distance had closed. "Johnny, I missed you!" I began. "I know it's only been a month since school let out and you left for camp, but it seems like a year. Like a whole, blasted year!"

"I just got in yesterday morning," John informed me, maneuvering his bike through our figure eight pattern on the hot asphalt. Riding and talking like this were two of our favorite pastimes. "I was gonna come over and see you this afternoon. I made something for you at camp, but it's at home. I'll get it for you later."

"Really?" I wondered aloud. "Really! For me?"

"But I didn't wrap it."

"That's okay. Wow, I really like gifts! How about a clue?"

"I'll just tell you what it is," he said.

"No. No, don't do that. You'll spoil it. No, I'll wait."

John tested his balance by taking both hands off the handlebars. Then he proudly folded his arms and continued to peddle. "Did you get your report card?" he asked. "I just saw mine yesterday. How'd you do?"

"Not so hot. I went down something awful the second half of this year. You knew that. But I hope to make a comeback this fall. I hear eighth grade isn't so hard. How about you? What did you end up with? As if I didn't know."

"Straight *A*'s," he boasted. "Straight *A*'s in everything all year!"

"Blechhh!" I returned and shook my head as I darted purposefully in front of him. Instinctively he grabbed the bike's handlebars. "I knew you would, Johnny. You always get *A*'s. Sure you should be seen with me?"

"Oh, for a little while," he teased and looped around to face me. He suddenly grew serious and asked, "How are things, Jeanie? You know, at home?"

I braked the pedals, then hopped my feet along the black pavement. When John saw I'd stopped to talk he followed my lead. "Johnny? Johnny, I have the most wonderful news!" I exclaimed and turned to face him directly. "I wanted to write you about it but I couldn't get your address. Johnny? It's heaven now!"

"What do you mean?" he inquired. "*What's* heaven?"

"*My father's moved out!* It's all over! The divorce was final just after the last week of school! He's gone! It was a total surprise, John. He finally moved out last month and I love it!"

"Oh."

"Is that all you got to say? *Oh?* What kind of a friend are you?"

"Oh, that's all."

"You should be jumping up and down for me. I've never been this happy, Johnny. Not ever."

"Well, don't you think you'll miss him?"

"Who? My father?"

"Yeah."

"Are you kidding?" I threw out my hands to dismiss the idea. "Thought I'd go right through the ceiling with joy when I watched him carry out his stuff. He still comes around to mess with things in the garage, but the last four weeks have been heaven. I'm not joking, either. He didn't leave without a fight, but he's gone. Really gone!"

John rubbed his hands over the chrome tubing on his bike. After a moment he continued, "I still think you'd miss him. I know I would."

"It's different, Johnny. You never knew your dad too well before he died. You think every kid wants a father as bad as you? It's not that way. Having no daddy is better than having one who hates you. It was awful, believe me. I'll never miss him. Never. I'd bet my life on it. And you know what? It'd suit me fine if I never saw him again. That's the truth, Johnny. I'd never lie to you."

"But at least you have one. Least you have a father."

"You are crazy, Johnny. You know that? *Crazy!* How many times do I got to tell you? He hated me. He was mean. Inside here," I broke away to touch my chest, "he hurt me over and over and over. I was afraid of him. I still am. Johnny, it was like hell, but now it's over. Finally I can sleep. Haven't had a nightmare in two full weeks. Two weeks! Finally I can look up and see a blue sky." I raised my eyes upward. "I'm not as afraid to go home anymore. I'm not as afraid to leave. It's got to be like heaven. I can't put it into words."

Johnny looked puzzled and kicked a pebble with his brown leather sandal. He did not comment.

"Listen to me. You think heaven is having a father, right?" I asked.

I pulled my fingers through the spray of pink handlebar streamers as I waited for his response. Finally he nodded yes. "Well, I'm telling you heaven is not having one. Do you understand? I'm free! I think I'm going to make it now. I never figured I could hang on this long, but it's all over. No more problems."

I paused and watched for any expression on John's face. "Well, at least say something, Johnny. Say *something*."

"Okay. Race you to Snyder's bridge!" he yelled, changing the subject.

"All right. All right, you're on, buddy. I can take on the world today!" I shouted and mounted my seat. "Watch, Johnny, cause I'm gonna whip the socks off of you! Loser has to wash the other's bike, wheels and all, with a spit-polish shine. Got that?"

"You're dreaming if you think you're going to beat me," he challenged.

"Oh, yeah? Huh!"

"Huh to you!" John returned and wheeled his bike beside mine.

"You ready?"

"Call it, Jeanie. Go ahead."

"Okay. Ready. Set. *Go!*" I screamed and spun off. "I'm free! I'm in heaven! Watch me go, Johnny. Watch me! No hands!" I hollered and pointed to the clouds above.

"And heaven?" I continued. "You just keep smiling on me. I'm gonna win this race. I'm gonna win!"

The summer wind carried my blond strands fluttering over my shoulder as I pulled far ahead. Nothing could stop me now. Nothing.

8

Cross Fire

JEANIE, YOU HAVEN'T said a word in the ten minutes you've been here. What's wrong? Why all the tears? What's bothering you?

Everything.

Here. Use these. You can keep the box right there. Help yourself.

Everything's wrong. Nothing's right. I hate life, Dr. Willis. I hate it. I hate it. Why was I ever born? Do you know?

Try to relax, okay? Relax, Jeanie. Relax. That's it. Sit back. Take a deep breath.

I'm not going to make it.

Make what?

Life is too much. I can't handle it. I feel like I'm going down for the third time. Off the deep end. I'm not going to make it.

Can you be specific? Why are you crying so hard? What happened?

A lot of things.

Tell me about them. That's why I'm here. What has happened since I saw you last? I thought things were looking up for you a month or two ago.

It's Popcorn.

Your cat, right?

My cat. My very favorite thing in the whole world. Yeah, my cat.

Jeanie, try to relax. You're sobbing. Try to relax.

He's dead. Popcorn's dead. I came home with Christine from the store a couple nights ago. We pulled in the drive. I saw Peter go around the back of the house. Popcorn was dead. Peter had him on a shovel and was taking him out back to bury him. Popcorn was all I had, and now he's dead. He's dead. Popcorn's dead. He's dead and I'll never see him or play with him again. He's all I ever had.

Jeanie? Jeanie, relax.

But why did he have to die? Why? Why? Why did he get sick all of a sudden? Why? God must really hate me. It's probably my fault He took Popcorn. Anything that's good He's got to take away from me.

Jeanie, look at me. Take in a deep breath. Try to hold it. Let it out slowly. Let's do it again. Take it in. Hold it. That's good. That's good.

I miss Popcorn. I took care of him and loved him with all my heart. I did, Dr. Willis. I loved him and he loved me back.

What day did this happen?

Thursday or Friday, I can't remember for sure. I try hard not to think about him but everywhere I look there's something that brings him to my mind. The way he played with me. Where he slept on my bed. How he'd meow to be fed whenever I went near the kitchen. I just start crying all over again. Can't stop sometimes.

Do you have any other pets?

No. Bernie has a dog, but I always loved cats. My mother says I just got too attached to this one. To Popcorn. There'll never be another cat like him.

Jeanie, you're crying hard again. Remember? Relax. Try to relax for me. Try real hard.

Even if I had another cat it'd never take Popcorn's place. He meant everything to me. Why do you think God took him away? God's just like my father, you know. Anytime I start enjoying anything He's got to stop it. Destroy it. I think they both hate me. I think they both want me miserable. They get their kicks that way. I never pretended to like my father, and now? Now I don't like God. I don't want anything to do with Him. Not ever. No God of love would put me in this mess, and I don't just mean taking Popcorn away. I mean giving me life, if you can call it that. Maybe I was born to die. You know, a slow death where I die some each day? Here. Inside. God, can You hear me up there? I hate you back!

Jeanie? Jeanie? Relax. Relax now. Can you hear me? Relax. Let's just sit quietly for a minute or two, okay? Don't try to talk.

Now, Jeanie, look at me, please? All of this anger and hurt can't be just for Popcorn. What else has been happening? What's been going on at home since June? You were happy and laughing and feeling so much better when we talked then. What's going on at home? What's happened the last month or two at home?

Home?

Home.

I don't have a home, Dr. Willis.

Oh?

I live in a house but it's not home. Home is where you want to be.

Tell me what's happening there.

For the first month after the divorce I thought everything was getting better every single day. My father would hang around in our garage now and then, but that was it. Then my mother started inviting him in. Inside to eat. Or inside to fix the washer. She started doing things for him like sewing or baking him something special. We've always had trouble as long as I can remember with our pump, the electricity and wiring, the furnace—you name it—so now he's there almost every time I turn around. He says he's fixing things, but I bet it's his excuse to get inside.

Are you out of tissues? Here's a new box. Jeanie, how do you feel about your dad stopping by so much?

How do you think I feel? I never wanted anything to do with him. I hate it when he's there. I go to my room or I slip outside. Sometimes I go to the woods, climb trees, and cry all over again. Just like before. Except before I had the hope that the divorce would end it all. Now what's there to hope for? Huh? Where's the hope now? Do you know?

He's not stopped his drinking, I can tell you that. By accident I found him in the garage a couple weeks ago and he was drinking straight from a bottle. He about choked when he saw me. I just ran out as fast as I could go. Anything to get away from him. And my mother? I think she actually wants him back. Can you believe it?

So things are not so good with you and your mother now?

You said it! Why does she want him to come back? I argue with her all the time. She says what she does is none of my business and I'm too young to understand. If it's none of my business then why does it hurt me so much? I don't trust anybody. Not my father. Not my mother. Not anybody. It makes me want to throw up. And I do sometimes. I thought this was all over but it's not.

You want to hear the topper? I heard her on the phone last week telling him that she thought Bernie and I needed to see him more often! Can you believe it! Bernie's never home and I can tell you my father's the last person I'd ever want to see. When she got off the phone she told me Father wanted to visit me more often, too. I don't believe a word of it! And she's made me go with them a couple times out to eat. Like we're some kind of ideal little family now.

I ask you: where does a kid go to be alone? To get out of the cross fire? That's what I'd like to know. Where does a kid go to get divorced from his family? From everything? It feels like I'm on a roller coaster up and down all the time. I either feel ignored or used. Lately I'm being used and I can tell it. I don't think my mother gives a whit about me. She only wants him back. For what reason, I don't know and I don't care. But I tell you the truth, Dr. Willis. I'll run away if he moves back. I'll run so far no one will ever ever *ever* find me again. I'll kill myself before I live with him. I will.

Is that all you can do is sit there and shake your head? What are counselors for anyway? Can you bring back Popcorn? Can you get me out of this mess? Can you make the pain go away? You got an eraser big enough to do it?

Jeanie, if I shake my head it's because everything seems so complex right now for you. I understand why you're confused. I do. You're caught in the middle.

Yeah, in the cross fire. Tell me about it. Tell me about the hell inside, too. As if I didn't already know. You wonder why I don't think I'm going to make it? Tell me what I have to hold on to anyway. Church was out a long time ago. God's out. I wonder if I ever had any support in my family. Sure don't trust anyone there. My best friend tries but he can't understand. And now Popcorn. He's all I had. He's all I ever had. Now I'm alone. All alone.

Shh. Let's quiet down again, Jeanie. Let's breathe deeply and relax. Come on, please? Try to breathe in really deep this time. Try to stop crying so hard.

I know this probably doesn't sound like much comfort right now, but I care that this is such a difficult time for you. Do you see that plaque on my shelf beside you? It has four words on it, but they're words you need to remind yourself of over and over. Look at them, Jeanie. Let them soak in. Say them with me, "This too will pass."

You aren't feeling strong right now but you've stood in the midst of this two- or three-year storm. There's been a storm going on outside of you for a long, long time. But you and I know there's been another storm just as real. The one inside. You've withstood them both. You've survived.

This will pass. Storms pass, Jeanie. They don't stay forever. You've got to hang on. You can't give in. Not now. Not after all the winds and rain and lightning you've withstood. They will pass. Not overnight. But they will pass.

I'm going to put you back on the medication right away, okay? And I mean as soon as you get home and have some lunch. Do you understand?

Uh-huh.

Is your mother waiting outside?

I think so.

I'd like to see if we couldn't persuade her to consider letting you get a kitten. Would you like that?

You . . . you know I would.

Jeanie, your mother called me the day after Popcorn died. She said you were terribly upset and that she didn't know what to do. We can't change everything for you, but I think a new little kitten would be in order here.

I . . . I don't mean to sound ungrateful, Doctor, but I won't believe it until I see it. I don't trust anyone anymore. It's just the way I am. Talk with her. Please talk with her and do what you can. Try. But I'm not going to put my hope in getting a kitten *or in anything else in life* until I can see it and touch it. That's the way it's going to be from now on. That's the way it has to be.

I see.

Want me to send her in now?

Yes. And Jeanie? Remember that this too will pass.

For my sake I hope you're right.

It will.

I hear you.

So long. See you in a few days.

Yeah. So long and all that.

This too will pass.

I won't believe it until I see it. No more. I refuse to believe it.

Good-bye.

Yeah.

PART II

LOVE REGAINED

For my father and my mother have orsaken me, but the Lord will take ne up.

Psalm 27:10

Resurrection Plea

O God,
can You behold
my inner blindness?
That horrible
black-pitched
sunrise and sunset
of each day's eternity?
And can You hear
the savage cries explode
from the void and torment
as I crave
sense and sight?
O God,
are You there?
Do You care?
Then fold Your hands
around my own
quickly
tenderly
and spell Your life
and pulse Your light
into the deep wasteland.
Renovate,
O God,
and set free.
Restore the broken image
in me.

9

Civil War

I YAWNED SO WIDE that my jaw cracked with a bony *pop* as I checked the color of my complexion in the rear-view mirror. Leaning away from the steering wheel I focused my eyes on the rectangular glass fixture centered along the windshield brim. Perhaps others in my world did not know the truth about me, but I did: anxiety and fatigue followed me wherever I went. Whether in school or out of school. At work. At home. Day or night. Wherever. Whenever. They were my constant companions. I could tell it in my tired eyes as I glanced in the rear-view mirror that cold morning, and I could tell it in my restless soul.

I sat quietly a moment to reflect. One thing I'd learned for sure in my eighteen years was that there were definitely two types of rear-view mirrors. Anyone could handle and adjust the glass, oblong kind like the one hanging inside my car. But the second kind, invisible to everyone but me, was housed only in my thoughts, and it was much more difficult to adjust. No matter how much I tried and clawed and fought to go forward in life, that inner mirror continually reflected a thousand memories of yesterdays. Hurtful memories. Depressing ones. They were always there. Always lurking in the shadows of today. Always distorting my vision of tomorrow.

I grabbed between the gray bucket seats for my sketch folder and books. Taking one last glance in the mirror, I sighed heavily and thrust open the door. After double-checking my pockets for the ring of silver keys, I sealed up the old red VW. Even though my watch was at home, I could tell by the number of empty automobiles parked around me that I was minutes behind schedule for my eight o'clock class. Somehow I didn't care. Caring would take too much effort.

Instead I walked slowly and looked overhead to see the faded white sky. All nature's signs pointed to the obvious fact that winter was not far off. Of the four seasons I had always disliked winter the most. The icy snow. The chilling cold. The brittle, glasslike scenery that always reminded me of death. The morning and evening darkness. "Brrrr," I said and pulled up the collar of my jacket against the crisp November morning. Clutching my books closely, I proceeded toward the science building entrance.

"You're late, Campbell," Professor Shivers observed without looking directly at me or at the wooden door.

"Yes, sir," I mumbled and slid into a vacant seat near the back of the room. I unzipped my red nylon jacket and fastened it around the outside of my chair as Dr. Shivers continued his lecture from forty feet away. His ability to identify tardy students without pausing to glance at them always amazed me. He must have had a sixth sense about it. That, or he had a special skill cultivated by years of deliberate analytical reasoning. Mathematicians were like that, I'd concluded. All of them. They were not flesh and blood beings, but unfeeling, mechanical calculators, void of life's deeper passions. They were robots. Human robots.

I'd taken advanced courses in mathematics all through high school, but the college I attended required freshmen to select at least one class from its logic department. All the names of the courses sounded terribly boring to me since my first loves had always been English, writing, and art, but I finally chose Algebra and Geometry Overviews I. I figured this particular class showed the greatest promise for abstract thinking, and it would refresh my memory of some not-too-distant topics.

I looked at the clock above the door and cleared my throat. Next I reached under my geometry text for my artist's notebook and flipped through a series of pencil outlines to find a blank sheet of paper. Drawing in my sketch pad probably seemed odd to a lot of people who sat nearby during any class, but it was perhaps my favorite pastime. It brought me a sense of pleasure and relaxation wherever I was. Besides, I didn't need my nose always stuck in the book or my eyes always toward the lectern.

For lack of anything better to do at exactly 8:17 that Wednesday morn, I decided to draw. I was never one for oceans or landscapes, although I had gone through a period of time two years earlier when I chose to design a collection of majestic trees. Today I wanted something exquisite and fragile. Something resplendent and delicate. Within a few seconds I decided to create my own crystal clock. A one-of-a-kind timepiece. Not like the mass-produced, drab institutional clocks that hung in every corner of the campus.

All kinds of clocks fascinated me. Time fascinated me, too, like the amount of time I'd already spent in college. I was nine weeks and three days into my freshman year and hating every minute of it. Was it the commuting back and forth from home? Was it working until eleven o'clock or later several evenings each week? I wondered. Was my unhappiness due to having come to this college in the first place when all my friends went to state universities? The very thought that I accepted a scholarship and grants to attend a Christian liberal arts college was revolting to me now. How I'd compromised! Students here seemed passive. Dull. Ultra-conservative. They were non-thinkers compared to the close band of impressive friends I'd clung to in high school. Did I hate this place so much because I longed to be back with them again? Back with my creative, sophisticated friends? I was a stranger here. And I hated all the mentions of God and chapel and purpose and on and on. I hated all of it. I did not belong here, and I was tired of pretending like I did.

Shivers's voice cut through my drawing and dreaming. "Miss Campbell?" he asked. I put down my pencil and looked up to see the instructor brush his mustache with his lower lip.

"Sir?" I replied.

He clicked the small white piece of chalk against the green surface of the board beside him. "We're waiting to hear your wisdom on the subject."

"Sure," I answered in a cocky tone of voice. "What would you like to know?" My arrogance was the outward expression of my personal rebellion at being in this class and at this school. But on a much deeper level and for a much longer period of time, it had become my best disguise to hide the hurting person inside. Not too many people would bother to cut through the density of my smoke screen, I'd discovered. It was easier for them, and for me, if they kept their distance.

"We were discussing this proof," Dr. Shivers announced.

"And?" I returned matter-of-factly.

"*And* we're wondering how you'd go about analyzing it."

"Okay," I stated and quickly glanced at his blackboard scribble. My heart was racing, yet I strained to project an air of overconfidence.

"Okay. We're given the fact that *y* squared equals eleven *k*. We're also given the fact that *k* is an element of *z*. If you want to solve or prove that *y* equals eleven *p*, *p* is an element of *z*, then I guess there are two possibilities. Better write these down," I said to Dr. Shivers and paused for him to stretch out his arm.

"First," I continued, "consider alpha. We have *y* equal to eleven *p* and *p* is an element of *z*. Secondly . . . secondly, beta. With beta, *y* is not equal to eleven *p*, *p* is an element of *z*. So let's assume beta holds. Then these steps would follow.

"One? *Y* squared is not equal to one hundred twenty one *p* squared. It follows that *y* squared is not equal to eleven *m*, *m* equals eleven *p* squared. With the assumed beta, this would be given in order for beta to hold true."

I waited long enough to stare directly at my instructor. He hardly *ever* let students prove an entire problem alone. Why wasn't he calling on someone else by now? I was annoyed but forced myself to go on in deliberate staccato rhythm.

"Two? *Y* squared is not equal to eleven *p*, but since *y* squared equals eleven *k* and *k* is an element of *z* were both given, the next statement must hold true: *y* squared equals eleven *p*. Three? Since a statement that is given cannot be both equal and not equal at the same time, beta leads to a contradiction. And four? Alpha is what remains." I stopped, folded my arms and informed, "I'm through."

To my surprise Dr. Shivers bounced the chalk in his opened palm and directed another question my way. "Miss Campbell? What do you think is the most fundamental element that we must grasp before solving geometric proofs of any kind?"

"Of any kind?" I repeated. I glanced to my right and left and forward through the faces watching mine. Why did I feel like I was on trial here? Why did I feel so defensive? "Well, if you want my personal philosophy, I'd have to say the most fundamental fact, sir, is that given information always holds true. It never changes. It always stays the same. Always. It will hold true until hell freezes over." I threw in the last phrase for shock value. Not for me and not for Dr. Shivers, but for the students who sat so calmly around me day after day. They were never ruffled. Never caught off guard.

"Very good," Dr. Shivers noted. "Very good. Class, let's take a moment and look again at the absolute truth of given facts. They are not assumptions on which we build. *We must consider them truths.* Take, for example, this next problem."

He wheeled around to scratch new letters, numbers, and brackets for us to see. By the time he was into his next sentence I was off again, withdrawn into my own world of drawing and thinking. Periodically I glanced up to the board to at least give the outward appearance of interest, but I knew I was safe the rest of this class. Shivers would not call on me again.

I wondered what all this talk of givens and truths was for in the first place. Was it simply intellectual rhetoric? Had anyone's life ever been restored by theorems and postulates? I chuckled as I drew the shiny base of my crystal clock. I could just imagine a woman rushing to a doctor in mortified terror. "Doctor! Doctor! My son! His eyes are glassy and he's choking to death! He's going to die!" And I could just imagine the wonderful doctor calmly asking her if she understood that planes running parallel through infinity never touched. She answers, "Yes! I see it now! Oh, Doctor! That's it! You've saved him! You've saved my son!" Fat chance of that happening, right? Then what was all this algebraic and geometric nonsense for anyway?

"Given information always holds true," I silently reviewed. "It is the most fundamental fact upon which everything builds." Everything builds on given information? I considered what it would be like to have my life analyzed mathematically. If my puny existence were plastered all over Shivers' green board, where would he begin to solve it? How could he make sense of a senseless life? What could he assume about my future based upon the givens of my past?

I stopped my pencil swirls and lines and squinted my tired eyes. Shivers was still going on hot and heavy, pointing with his smaller-than-ever chalk to a particular group of numbers along the far side of the board. How could he be so intense about this kind of absurdity? I didn't like Shivers. Not at all. In fact, with all my heart I wanted to stand up and shout, "Hey, buddy? Why don't you straighten your stupid tie? Huh? Why don't you get a decent piece of chalk, too, for crying out loud? And why don't you do something useful for a change and figure out what I'm doing here? Huh? Here in life! Why don't you scribble out a dozen of your damn proofs for me? Why don't you tell me why the hell I was born? Do you think you could do that? Do you think you could figure out who I am? And how I had the awful, disgusting luck to land in *your* class with all these depthless morons? Can you do it, buddy? Can you?"

I paused as the movie scenario continued in my mind. "Oh? You want some of my *own* givens? Gladly! I say let's start at the beginning.

Get these down, all right? Given: a baby girl is born and the first human contact she receives is a smack from her good old doctor. Given: she starts crying and that sound continues to echo years and years later. Given: she does whatever kids do until she's eight or ten, and then *boom!* There's trouble on the old home front. Given: she's alone and feels abandoned by everyone as her mother and father battle it out before, during, and after the divorce. Given: this young girl learns during her teenage years that there are a thousand new definitions to the word *games*.

"You want more, Shivers? We could be here all day, but let's go ahead and see where this leads, okay? Given: the games don't stop even after her father remarries or after her mother faces some serious health problems. Given: did I mention the crying and tears? There are lots of them, Doc Shivers, and there are lots of court hearings and trials and setbacks that follow. Given: somehow the girl survives on high school activities, a handful of friends, and her dream to write. She certainly looks respectful on the outside—a real churchgoer and award collector—but very clever. And very cocky. You see, by now she's learned to play quite a few games herself, and play them well. Given: steadily through the years she's become more and more infuriated inside at life. She's bitter. She's broken. She loathes herself. And she despises God with every fiber of her eighteen years. In short, she seethes with anger day and night, and her rage is about to burst wide open all over the place.

"Well, I guess that about sums it up," I imagined myself saying. "What do you make of it, Shivers? Pretty complex, isn't it? A royal mess. But give it your best shot. Put all your logical reasoning behind the muck and tell me what's ahead for me based on my past given facts that never change. Tell me how long. How long, sir? How long before I self-destruct? A week? A month? A year? How long do you give me? Or should we be thinking in terms of minutes and hours? Will I make it through today? Maybe I'll self-destruct right here in your presence. I want to, do you know that? I want to detonate and explode into smithereens and be done with everything. Think I'll find peace then? I doubt it. *I doubt if I'll ever find peace.*"

The scenario was over. Almost every daydream concluded at the same point of despair, but somehow I'd never gotten used to the sad endings. Defeated again, I bowed my head to hide the pools of tears that formed and slid over my hot cheeks. I slowly pulled off my glasses with one hand and covered my forehead with the other. I used my fingers and thumb to massage my wet eyelids, knowing very well the tears would continue to spill out. I needed to leave the room before people noticed. I could not bear the thought of patronizing smiles or puzzled expressions of concern. No, I needed to gather everything, grab hold of the metal doorknob that was so near to my seat, and flee to some place of temporary refuge. Perhaps to the woman's lounge downstairs, but I needed to hurry. Hurry fast.

Maybe it was just from fatigue after crying so hard in the lavatory annex where I rested by myself, but I was aware of an unusual lighting effect that seemed to encircle me in the small room. In fact, the atmosphere within those four walls was mysteriously strange to me. Eerie. I examined the lounge in fearful wonder. There were no ceiling lamps above me to cast such wide patches of theatrical, high-contrast shadows to my half of the annex, only a narrow string of fluorescent tubes that stretched across the rectangular wall mirror. From them came irregular yellowish beams that shimmered off the shiny surface into the nearby corners.

I glanced down at the pile of crumpled, damp tissues in my lap and then back at the mirror on the opposite wall. By comparison to the brightly illuminated looking-glass, I seemed to sit in total darkness. How odd. Even fireworks against an ebony sky would not have displayed more contrast than did the mixture of light and dark images in the small waiting room. And if this setting around me were not bizarre enough, my face actually shone in the mirror like an overexposed picture. I knew I was tired but I wasn't dreaming all of this. The atmosphere around me was vividly real, and my bleached facial reflection was dramatically real, too. Then why could I not make any sense of it? None whatsoever?

I closed my sore eyes against the morning confusion and forced myself to take in several deep breaths. How grateful I was to be alone and unbothered. Even though eight o'clock classes were to dismiss soon and students would quickly fill the halls upstairs, I'd thought ahead and intentionally chosen the women's lounge in the furthermost catacombs of the basement level to give me the greatest assurance of privacy. Not many students would take the effort to come here between classes, especially so early in the day.

My mind and body ached for hours of sweet, forgetful escape. Part of me wanted to pull up my knees, fall back into the recess of the pale orange couch, and go to sleep forever; but another part of me realized

I had to get on with the business of survival. Experience had taught me that if I let depression get the better of me so early in the morning, the rest of the day would be a downhill trip—and I certainly couldn't handle descending any further. My emotions were already stretched to capacity.

Why did I always ponder life in moments such as these? When I was all too tired and all too depressed? I hated life. I really, really hated it. Everyday thousands of people died who had probably begged for life. Good people. Bad people. Rich. Poor. All colors. All ages. Some with careers and glorious destinies and happy, plump children. Many without food, family, or even the barest essentials. Those in horrible pain. In my mind's eye I could just see a thousand different people begging the Almighty for one more chance. One more go-round with life. One more gasp of air or gulp of food. And here I sat. Not a decent thought in my head. Not one iota's wish to continue my existence. With food and clothes and intelligence and creativity and hints of future promise. All neatly combined in one eighteen-year-old package. But as far as I was concerned? All of it could go to hell and I could go with it. I would never beg for life. I would never beg to continue something as meaningless and futile as life. Sartre, Ionesco, Beckett and all those other playwrights to whom I'd clung were much closer to the truth: life was an absurdity. An existential, second-class absurdity. A nonsensical journey bound for nowhere. Who would beg for more of *that?* Not I. I might beg and argue for death, but I would never argue for life. Never in a million years. I hated life.

In the midst of my private civil war came a startling interruption. My eyes flashed in disbelief to discover three young women storm into the lavatory annex. Their combined weight bolted against the metal door, smacking it against the adjacent concrete divider. Everything in the small room shook. The walls. The couch on which I sat. Even the fluorescent lights flickered above the mirror. The force of impact jerked the youthful trio back across the opened threshold while the door loudly reverberated on its hinges. Waves of laughter rippled from the little band of intruders as they fumbled to launch ahead. When they stumbled past me toward the door leading to the toilets and sinks, I saw the third girl raise a can of dessert whipped cream over her head. The other two were obviously fleeing past me to escape a foamy attack.

"Infants!" I thought. "Nothing but college infants playing chase with their blasted whipped cream at nine o'clock in the morning. Why don't they just grow up?"

In a matter of seconds the third girl had won the greatest advantage. She whirled up from behind, kicked her legs past the others, and thrust her foot against the inner door so it could not be pulled open. The two helpless girls in front of her squeezed and jerked the aluminum handle, but to no avail. The door would not budge. Up went the long slender red-and-white can of cream in the third girl's hand, and out spurted a runny trail of liquid foam. From behind, she splattered the hair and shoulders of her two captives and laughed wildly in victory.

"Let's get out of here!" one of the victims shouted as she turned around and wiped some cream directly from her shoulder onto the glasses of her attacker.

"Right!" the other agreed wholeheartedly.

For a moment all three lost their balance, then recklessly dodged sideways to retrace their steps. I protectively swung my legs aside after one pointed shoe jutted sharply into my ankle during the scuffle.

"What relief!" I thought when I realized they were heading back out into the hallway from which they'd mysteriously come instead of into the inner recesses of the women's lounge.

Somehow the two cream-covered youths managed to be in the lead again as they clawed at the doorknob to depart. In their excitement, however, they kept the door from opening. When they eventually had the good sense to step backward, the door gave way at once. Just like before, it crashed inwardly against the concrete wall and caused everything in the room to rattle. Everything. As the laughing duo vanished, the third girl paused long enough to wipe the cream from her glasses.

"Don't leave on my account!" I sighed under my breath.

I'm not sure if the remaining partner heard my comment or not, but she turned toward me and uttered apologetically, "Sorry about this, but those two have been driving me *crazy* with pranks!" Then she stepped into the hall, glanced both right and left, and furiously shook her can of whipped cream. As a courteous afterthought, she hastily clutched the sticky doorknob and unintentionally jerked it much too hard behind her. The door smacked shut with such compelling force that I jumped two inches. The tubular lights flashed off, then on, and the floor literally shook.

"Thank God they're gone!" I said while clutching my chest in amazement.

Before I had time to blink my eyes, there came from the mirror a dull, quick sound, like distant thunder warning of the onslaught of a terrible storm. "What on earth!" I exclaimed as I sprang to my feet to draw closer to the source of the noise. As I gazed into the mysterious, light-dark mirror, I couldn't believe what was happening. Never before in my entire life had I seen anything like it.

Webbing out from one of the clear plastic rosette supports along the far left edge of the mirror were brilliant tinsel strings. They cracked. They crossed. They spread further and further out. Apparently the vibrations of the concrete wall jolting against the mirror were too much for it to bear. Like rivers leading into the ocean, the luminous fragile lines slowly continued their jagged journey. I witnessed all this in dumfounded surprise.

"Stop!" I whispered, touching my palm gently against the glass surface. "Please stop!" I knew if the lightning cracks inched their course fully to the opposite side, the entire mirror would tumble away from the wall. Thousands of pieces would fragment at my feet.

I held my breath. I waited. I sweated. By now both my hands were tactfully pressed against the mirror's surface. How could I ever explain this? Who would believe that one minute I was resting and minding my own business, and all of a sudden the room was bombed by three cream-bearing students I didn't even know? And after the last one left, the mirror began to disintegrate? Who would believe me? And how could I ever afford to pay for a huge lavatory mirror? A mirror I didn't even break.

"Oh, God, make it stop," I pleaded. To my relief the silver-green hairs dead-ended of their own accord a good foot and a half from the right-hand border.

"Whew!" I sighed. "And now to get my junk and get the hell out of here!"

Tediously I stepped backward and delicately, delicately pulled my fingertips away from the mirror. I had no trouble with the right hand, but a triangular piece of glass stuck to my left thumb and came out from the wall. I could not catch it before it crashed into twenty little diamond chips, giving off a high-pitched tinkling sound. I gasped and glanced back to the space from which the piece had come. Perhaps more glass bits would fall now that the inner boundaries had been disturbed. I stood motionless. Only a half-inch sliver of ice gave way above the vacant spot, and that was the end of the glassy avalanche.

Hopefully the mirror would stay intact as long as nothing else quivered against the wall surface.

With my eyes fixed ahead I suddenly thought of Alice's own little Wonderland and her magical looking-glass. Is this what it was like for her? Is this how her journey through time and space began?

"Alice?" I said out loud. "Alice, your glass wasn't broken. But look at mine. Look if you dare."

Instead of backing away from the mirror, I drew closer. There, directly in front of me and brilliantly clear, was the black-white reflection of my own fractured image. I looked intently at the disjointed portions of my face. An eye slightly turned one way. Parts of my cheekbone protruding out. My chin elongated. My forehead blurred and partially missing. My eyebrows irregular, swerved in concave distortions. Hair shafts zigzagging back and forth. Yes, my facial image—just like my badly damaged life within—was anything but harmonious, whole, or congruent. It was far more than disunited. It was totally broken. Severely shattered. Just like me inside. Exactly like me inside.

There, captured on the silvery shafts of cracked glass, I saw the sorrow and disappointment and ruin and struggles of my inner life. "Mirrors can be replaced," I heard myself cry in the empty room, "but who can replace you, Jean Campbell? Who? Who can take this piece and that piece and all the pieces lost somewhere in your past and bring them back together again? Who can take the hurt away? Who can make you whole?"

I did not bother to dash away the trails of tears tumbling down my cheeks. "You better face the facts, kid," I uttered harshly, thrusting out a pointed finger toward the mirror's surface. My voice trembled as I continued, "You're a first class loser, do you know that? And if you don't get some help fast, you're going to die. Do you hear me? You're going to self-destruct and you're going to die. You know you will. You've tried everything you know to relieve the ache inside, and you need help, Jean Campbell. Soon. Or it'll be too late. You'll self-destruct. You'll die. You will."

Panic seized me because the words had been spoken. Spoken by my own mouth. They were truth. They were the *given facts upon which everything else must build.* I knew deep in my soul that the words I prophesied were truth. Absolute truth.

I forced myself backward to break the chains of my shadowy spell, and I heard and felt the crystal chips grind to finer particles under both my shoes. Still watching the awful, light-dark vision in the mirror, I fumbled for my books and coat on the couch behind me. I was scared to death. Petrified. I must be gone. I must race against this day and this mirror and this inner storm and be gone. I must get to the car. Anywhere. Just away. I was a loser and I was going to die. I knew it clearly now. Me. Jean Campbell. I was going to die. And if something didn't happen to change me fast, I knew it would be soon. The fragments inside me were falling too rapidly to catch anymore. I was coming apart—shattering at the seams—and I knew it. Today with all my heart I knew it.

I slipped into the empty hallway and closed my eyes so tightly they hurt. As I paused to inhale a deep, deep breath, my fear transformed into spite. With growing resentment I slammed the door as hard as I could. I listened. When the sound of distant glass-thunder echoed through the metal divider, I knew for sure it was time to go.

10

Surrender

MY HAND WAS poised in mid air. For the longest time I stood outside Miss Yarger's faculty office and debated. Had I journeyed across the cold campus for nothing? Would this simply be another exercise in futility or would I have the courage this time to knock?

I waited as the wooden door vibrated on its hinges, echoing my decision. I tried again, this time harder. I did not want to appear too eager, yet I knew in my heart I had reached a new level of desperation. Where else could I go now? Who else would take me in and listen?

"Well, hi, Jean," the youthful English teacher said as she swung the door wide open to her tiny office. She motioned for me to sit down beside her desk, then grabbed for the telephone to continue her conversation. I stopped to close the door behind me and overheard Miss Yarger respond, "No, not tonight, Evelyn. I'm still trying to shake my cold. How about the day after tomorrow around five thirty?"

She paused for a reply while I slid nervously onto the pale green fiberglass chair and thought of a hundred reasons why I shouldn't have come. "Tomorrow it is," I heard my instructor say. "See you then." Miss Yarger cradled the phone back in its place and stretched up to unfasten one of her golden earrings. She was blond, in her late twenties, and petite.

"You look troubled," she observed and glanced down at the piece of jewelry in her hand. "You didn't say a word in English today. That's unusual."

"I . . . well . . . I didn't feel much like talking."

We both waited in silence, then I stood hastily to my feet. "I guess it wasn't such a hot idea, my coming here and all. I'm sorry. You know me. So impulsive. Indecisive. I'll just go. I didn't mean to bother you. Besides, you've got a cold. You could use a break. We all could."

She coughed several times. I glanced back at her puzzled expression as I reached for the doorknob. "You're not bothering me," Miss Yarger stated and pulled a yellow lozenge from the small cardboard box on her desk. I watched her put the round disc in her mouth. She cleared her throat a third time and continued, "If you were bothering me I'd tell you. Why don't you sit back down and tell me what's on your mind?"

"But it doesn't have a thing to do with school or your class," I returned and looked once again toward the wooden door.

"So much the better," she replied. "Come on, Jean. Have a seat."

I nibbled at my lower lip. What would leaving Miss Yarger accomplish? Could I bear to go unchanged one more day? If there was even the slightest chance for relief, shouldn't I stay? Maybe, just maybe, she could help.

"If you're absolutely sure you're not busy," I uttered.

"Jean, I wouldn't say it if I didn't mean it. You're not bothering me."

"I . . . I don't even know where to begin," I stammered.

"You can begin by coming back and sitting down."

I scanned the doorway and then Miss Yarger. I wanted both to stay and to leave. I felt terribly uncomfortable. Terribly transparent. Like always in her presence I was stripped bare naked before her and I knew she was able to see right through me then. I knew she always could.

My fingertips tensely brushed over the doorknob and vanished into the pocket of my winter jacket. "I need help," I whispered. "I'm not going to make it."

"Make what?" came the concerned response. "Jean, why don't you sit down and tell me?"

I followed her directions and backed into the curve of the hard chair. At the most, Miss Yarger and I were now three feet apart. I could not bear to look her in the face as I tried to continue. "Life. I don't think I can hack it. It's just too big. I can't make it. I'm not going to survive. You? You're strong. You're *whole*. But I don't think I was ever meant to be. I can't go on. Not one more day. I can't."

"Jean, what's happened?" she questioned while I slipped off my winter coat. I felt like I was on fire. "Jean? How do you mean you can't go on?"

"Well, I just can't go on this way," I said and stared at the floor. "I'm tired. I'm so, so tired. Life tires me. School tires me. Breathing tires me. Miss Yarger, some people weren't meant to live." I deliberately paused and gulped to overcome the constriction of my throat muscles.

"And you're trying to say you are one of them?" Miss Yarger asked, clutching another Kleenex.

"I've . . . I've been running all my life. I can't run anymore," I anguished.

"Running?"

"Struggling," I explained. "Trying to float. But I'm telling you, I can't go on. Nothing's worth it. I'm drowning."

"Jean, you've shared bits and pieces of your searching with me before. Do you remember what I told you then?"

"But I hate God," I snapped. "I don't want anything to do with Him."

My instructor tossed her Kleenex into the wastebasket beside the desk. "Just for the record, why don't you review with me why it is you hate God?"

I stroked my chin in shame. My lips quivered, and I knew I was close to tears. "I guess everything boils down to the fact that God hates me. If He loved me, why didn't He help me? He's had a million chances all my life. He made me into a nothing. A big zero. I was born that way. Inferior. You name it.

"If God cares about me at all it's only to see what I do wrong," I said quietly. "And let me tell you, Miss Yarger, there isn't one thing I do right. I'm not really smart. You think I am, but it's all an act. I'm not pretty. I'm absolutely broke all the time. I'm not even worth the air I breathe. I struggle just to get myself out of bed each day. I don't belong anywhere. I never have. I mean really belong. I'm alone. I miss my friends from high school something awful. I came to this college so I could commute and get my family off my back. A compromise. They wanted me to go to some Baptist university down South that was more like a Christian reformatory. My one brother goes there now and all he does is preach at me. He tells me how wrong I am. How off the track. I'm a sinner flying down some chute straight to hell as far as he's concerned. Nothing I do is right. I can't please anybody."

"Back to God," Miss Yarger interjected. "Why do you hate him?"

"Like I said, He hates me," I mumbled and looked down to my

lap. My fingers toyed nervously with a frayed thread from my brown sweater. "I'm some kind of a joke to God. Maybe you're worth helping, but me? I guess it's okay to Him if I struggle, struggle, struggle. God knows I've asked for His help enough, but do I ever get it? Not on your life. I ask for happiness. I ask to be a somebody to Him, but it's all in vain. I'm a nothing, Miss Yarger. A worthless nothing."

The young instructor reached for a cup of coffee I had not seen before. She took a swallow from the dark blue mug, glanced out the window, and squinted her eyes in thought. Turning toward me, she questioned, "How exactly could God help you? What would you want from Him to prove you are important? How could He help?"

"How?" I repeated, quite subdued. "How? He could try giving me a brand new inside. A whole new identity. Maybe zap me right out of existence for all I care. Or, better yet, He could take all the hurt away. Yeah, that's it. That's how He could help. He could take it all away." I stopped speaking to fight the lump in my throat.

"Jean, you feel like God has deserted you—"

"But hasn't He?" I broke through angrily. "Hasn't He?" I demanded again.

"You feel like God has deserted you," she reiterated slowly, "but you've survived. You've got strength many kids your age have never been forced to develop. That must count for something. You do have strength, Jean."

"Strength? You think I'm strong?" I spoke in amazement. "You've got to be kidding. Inside, deep inside, I'm probably the weakest kid on this campus. I'm not strong. Strong people can handle life. I'm a failure at everything I try." I stared at the ceiling. There was something painful about the words I uttered, but something healing. I had not confessed my thoughts aloud with this kind of openness in years.

"Are you a failure, Jean?" Miss Yarger eventually said to end the silence. "You earned an *A* in my course fall term and you tested out of another English course. That doesn't sound like failure to me. And don't you already have a few writing awards? How many freshmen here can boast of that kind of talent? You have a string of high school achievements as long as your arm. How can you say you're a failure? There's no evidence for that at all. How can you just dismiss everything like that?"

I rubbed my damp palms against my corduroys and redirected my attention to Miss Yarger's face. "All right, then, let me clarify what I mean. I'm a failure at things that really count in life. I'm a big zero.

Achievements are useless. And those awards don't mean a damn thing to me now. They're hollow. Empty. And you know something? *I'm hollow. I'm empty.* Maybe you think I'm kidding, but I can't go on. I've reached my limit. There isn't anything here worth sticking around for. Life is futile, futile, futile, Miss Yarger. For me it is. Like old Solomon said, 'Vanity, vanity, all is vanity.'"

Immediately Miss Yarger raised a finger to agree, "That's what Solomon thought, all right. But what else did he record in his search, Jean?"

"I guess I don't follow what you mean."

The instructor snatched a fresh Kleenex just in time to sneeze. "This cold!" she exclaimed and blew her nose. "Where was I?"

"Something about Solomon," I answered.

"Right," she stated. "Like you, Solomon tried and tried to find meaning to life. He figured if he'd accumulate a long list of accomplishments and belongings, then he'd be 'together'. He tried pleasure—all forms of worldly and sensual delights. When he found that pleasure didn't fill his emptiness he went onto possessions. Scripture records that he amassed the kind of wealth unequaled in history. When he found no satisfaction there, he pursued wisdom. He was known all around the world for his extraordinary intelligence. But there was still something missing inside. Did I mention his quest for power? And labors? Finally, at the long end of his journey and only after he had considered all the possible ingredients for happiness and purpose, he had nowhere else to go but to God. And do you know something, Jean? God was more than adequate to fulfill his deepest longings. Apart from God, all is vanity. That's what Solomon learned. 'Vanity, vanity, all is vanity.' That was absolutely true until he considered God.

"I suspect that you and Solomon are a lot alike. You've told me before all the things you've tried in your personal search. It doesn't surprise me that you've struck out. Believe me, you aren't alone. There's a whole world out there clamoring for power or wealth or pleasure or intelligence. Perhaps those things will tide them through the night, but morning always comes. The light exposes the emptiness all over again. I don't honestly believe any of those searchers will ever find what they're looking for apart from God. And as your friend, I honestly don't believe you will find what you're looking for apart from God either."

Miss Yarger touched my arm that rested on her desk top, and I intentionally jerked it away. "God, God, God," I said in disappoint ment. "Is that all you can talk about? Every time I come here you'v always got to bring Him into it. What am I? A masochist? You thin I like being the end result of His jokes? I need a God who can hel me with my problems, not give me more of them. I need a God c love, not some sadist who enjoys kicking me around."

She looked directly into my eyes and spoke softly, "God is love."

"Prove it," I challenged. "Prove He could ever love me." I thrus my index finger to my chest. "Me, Miss Yarger. All by myself. Prov He could ever love me."

Miss Yarger paused to reflect and then answered, "I can't exactly We have to rely on Scripture. Over and over it says God is a God o love, not hate. He doesn't play cruel jokes. He understands your hurts Jean, and He hurts right along with you. I wouldn't say that if I didn believe it with all my heart. I'm sure it grieves Him to see you tor up now just as it grieved Him to see you torn up back then. He give His creation free choice, and when we abuse our free choice we pa the consequences, which are often painful."

"Free choice?" I mumbled. "I didn't choose anything, so why shoul I have to bear the pain? My folks get off scott free and I'm left bearin the scars. You think I'd be over everything by now, but I'm still tor up. I hurt like hell. You're the first person I've told that to in years but it's the truth. I do hurt. All the time I hurt."

My teacher's eyebrows were furrowed together. I could tell sh was following every word I said. I could tell she tried to understand At last she spoke, "You work so hard at resisting God. It doesn surprise me you're thoroughly exhausted. Jean, if you never hear an other word I say, hear me now: God is love. He's the author of love Of all that's pure and good and wholesome. He loves *you*. Do yo understand? You are important. God loves you. Trust me."

"I want to, Miss Yarger. I want to, but I'm so afraid."

"Afraid of what?" she asked softly.

"I don't know exactly," I sighed. "I don't know. I guess afraid c God. Afraid if I give myself over to Him He'll destroy me completely Does this make any sense? I'm afraid He'll squelch any sign of life i me. That He'll make life twice the burden it is already by slappin rules on me that I just can't follow. Or He'll get some kick out c smashing all my dreams. Or He'll kill anything that means somethin to me.

"If I give myself over to God, I'll be just where He wants me. The *wham!*" I banged my fist on Miss Yarger's desk top. "*Wham!* He'll give it to me with both barrels. I guess I think He enjoys seeing me suffer. I'm afraid of Him, Miss Yarger. He scares me. I don't trust what He's up to.

"See, you think I matter to Him, don't you?" I waited for her response. "Don't you?" Only when she nodded yes, I added, "Well, you can think that if you want to, but me? How could I matter? He's got billions of little do-gooders running around all over the place, and you mean to tell me I can matter? *I'm a nobody!* Worthless. I could never matter like all His other kids. I could never matter like you. I can feature Him loving you. You're smart. You're beautiful. You come from a nice family. You've got your act together. You haven't screwed up your life."

Miss Yarger leaned back in her chair and posed, "And you have?"

I tried to laugh but couldn't. "Well, let's say I've had a lot of help along the way, but yeah. Yeah, I've screwed it up. I've jumped through hoops all my life to get accepted by people and even by God. I suppose at the other extreme, sometimes I've done some pretty wild things just to thrust my angry fist back in God's face. Sometimes I've been so infuriated at Him—absolutely livid—that I'd destroy Him if I had the chance. I've never felt hatred like I have since I started college last September. Here I am, straight out of high school, a freshman of six months, and all I do is seethe with hatred. Hatred for life and for myself. Hatred that I'm so damn inferior to everybody and so damn afraid all the time. But the big hatred goes to God. Hatred for all those years I cried out for help and got nothing in return. When I needed Him most, where was He? Too busy to get His great big old hands dirty with a young kid who's hurting all over the place. What else was I supposed to think except that I wasn't good enough for Him to bother with? Not good enough. You know, that's the story of my life. I've never been good enough for anybody."

It was time to stop talking and I knew it. Not only did I sense the growing panic inside, but I was spinning around in circles. Painful circles. The self-defeating circles of my past and present.

"Jean, let me say something here," Miss Yarger noted as though she thought I was going to continue. "How can I put this?"

She grew quiet and pulled herself closer to the desk and closer to me. "It may take years—even a lifetime—to sort through all these issues you've just raised. Our paths in life have been so different that I can only understand your upbringing by contrast, not by comparison.

"You are terribly hard on yourself, Jean. You demand perfection. And if you don't see perfection in others or attain perfection yourself, you tend to discount everything. I can spot it in your writing papers. If whatever you do isn't flawless, you reject it all. I think you do that with yourself. I think you refuse to accept Jean Campbell because she's imperfect. You reject everything about her. That's what I see you doing.

"I'm no psychologist, but I suspect that quite early in life you heard or thought you were worthless, and you've been telling yourself that lie a million times since. Or you thought God didn't want you, so you based your whole self-image on that misconception. And it is a misconception, Jean.

"I wish I could believe it for you, but I can't. I wish I could somehow prove it to you, but I can't do that either. God is love. He's the missing link inside of you. You know a lot about God but you don't know God experientially. There's a huge difference between those two positions. All the difference in the world. I question if you've ever invited Him to show you what He's really like. I question if you've ever invited Him inside."

"God can make the difference, Jean. Trust me. He can. He loves you. He wants you. Only He can fill the huge void." She paused again in order to give me a chance to speak. When I could not, and she saw me blinking back the coming tears, she whispered, "Jean? Maybe today's the day. Maybe today's the day you stop running from God. Maybe today's the day for a brand new beginning. Could this be the time you've waited for? To discover a brand new—"

With no warning whatsoever, I bolted up from the hard fiberglass chair, snatched my winter coat from the floor where it had fallen, and rushed toward the door. "I got to go, Miss Yarger." My voice was cracked and strained. "I've just got to get out of here. Pray. Please pray. I swear to you I don't think I'm going to make it."

In a flash I was out of her office and heading down the hallway toward the exit.

That afternoon I lay on my bed and stared through red, swollen eyes at the blank white ceiling. "Oh, God," I sobbed in the empty house, "I hate You! You've won, You know. I can't fight anymore. There's no more energy left to fight. I honestly cannot run one more step or go one more day. I've exhausted my strength. I've tried all I know to try. For years I've run with all the blasted fury I could muster up and I have lost the race. You win. I lose. Does that make You happy? Does it? Does the cry of my little defeat matter enough in Your great big world to make Your day? Does it?"

Tears streamed from the corners of my eyes, crossed over my ears, and fell onto the pillow already sodden with moisture. The mattress trembled beneath me as I wept. "It's Your choice, You know. You can spear me through right here and now, God. Old warriors did that when they conquered. I cannot resist even the tip of Your sword, so go ahead. Pin me here like some specimen against Your cutting board and do what You do. I quit. I resign. I lay me down. Today, February 13, I lay me down. I give up the fight. It's over. The fighting's over."

I had sensed inner heaviness and desperation in my past, but never like I experienced that moment. Never before had I felt so totally hopeless. So thoroughly helpless. My life was over. Right there and then I was somehow participating in the death of Jean Marie Campbell and I was powerless to resurrect her meager existence another day. I was finished.

Even in the total confession of my defeat, I found no release. Over and over Miss Yarger's words played in my mind like an endless tape recording. *"God is love,"* I heard her say. *"He's the missing link inside of you. Only He can fill the huge void. Maybe today's the day, Jean. Maybe today's the day . . ."*

I swung around to my left side and grabbed under the edge of my pillow for a drier tissue. "God, I cannot stand this torment. What do You want from me? Do You want me to admit I'm a lost, hellbound sinner? All right, *I am.* Do You want me to admit I can't make it? I've already said it a million times before. *I can't make it.* Do You want me to cough out words of love and tell You how much I want You? You know I'd just be lying. I can't say much in my favor, but You know I've never tried to lie to You. What I really want is to be left alone by everybody. Especially You. I'd like the war to cease. I'd like to rest in peace. Just once.

"So what do You want from me? A royal invitation to come in? I'm scared, God, I'm so scared. And I'm so confused. You frighten me. Is Miss Yarger right? Do You want me? Do You want to come in? Inside all this mess? Is that it? I don't know about that, God. I just don't know. I'm so scared.

"I think this is the only way I can put it and mean what I say: if You really are love, God, if You could ever love me, if Your love is healing and not destructive, if You could ever find something in me to salvage, then I guess I could invite You in. Do You hear me? Can You hear me? I've never been more serious, God. Do You know what I'm trying to tell You? Are you there? I guess I'm inviting You in if You want to come and if You want to help like Miss Yarger says You do. To make me livable. Not to kill me, though, or make life more miserable. But to restore me if there's anything left in me worth restoring. If I haven't destroyed it all.

"You must help me, God," I wept uncontrollably. "I have nothing but fear of You. And hate because all along I thought You hated me. Did You hate me, God? Do You now? I guess I never was a special prize for anybody, let alone You. I guess I never will be. I'm altogether worn out and useless. I can't go on. Not one more day. I can't go on.

"Can You hear me, God? Jesus? Can You hear? If You want me, if You're all that Miss Yarger says You are, then I give You me. Only break the mold that holds me in. If You really are love then set me free today to run toward You, God. Please, oh please, *let this be the day*. Amen."

11

Journey Into Nowhere

I ARCHED MY BACK and dug inside my pocket for the key ring that pinched against my leg. It was not the six or seven keys tucked in the fold of my jeans that brought discomfort, but the attached miniature hourglass. Most people I knew were content with initals in their key rings, or perhaps little bronze or gold symbols, or sayings etched in wood or plastic, but I fancied a petite hourglass. It reminded me that time was always changing, though I didn't find an abundance of comfort watching the white sand filter down through the minute opening in the glass day after day. True, outer facts were ever changing in my personal little world, yet the phantom pains of fear, hurt, and loneliness were permanent qualities. Qualities I had not learned to shake, with or without the passage of time.

On the chain were keys to my old red VW, to my mother's home from which I commuted to school, to the back door of a neighborhood store where I was employed, some keys to file cabinets, and one to the editor's office of the college literary magazine. With a sigh of dismissal I put the silver ring on the wooden seat beside me as I looked around. If I'd wanted to retreat and be left totally alone I had come to the perfect place. I would not be disturbed here. Not in an empty sanctuary in the middle of the day. Here I was temporarily plucked out of time to meditate, cry, sort, whatever. Here I was safe.

I glanced around at the empty pews in front of me and at the narrow strips of colorful, stained-glass windows along the right wall. I guess it was pretty unusual that I decided to come to a church for solace, especially one I had never before attended. Of the half-dozen churches within walking distance from the college campus, I found myself on the step of Temple of Jesus. I had no idea what denomination, if any, the church represented, and I didn't care. I only needed to be alone. More than anything I wanted to inhale the peacefulness of this sanctuary. I wanted to be alone with God. Draw close to Him. Understand something more of His presence. I came for strength. His strength to go on.

I slouched forward in the pew, placed my elbows on my knees, and rested my head in the cup of my hands. I closed my eyes. Like always I felt overwhelmed to find a place to begin in prayer. I took several deep breaths before I uttered, "Oh, God. Help me not to fall apart here. Help me not to come unglued. It's been over a year since I asked You into my life. I'm over a year old in Your family and I still don't understand anything. God, I need You now more than I've ever needed You. And I want You: that much I know for sure. But I'm confused. *I'm so confused.* How do I find you? Just You? How do I know You? How do I shed the past and go on? How, God? Please, won't You—"

I stopped abruptly when I heard the creaking hinges of the large sanctuary doors behind me. I'd received permission from the church secretary to sit here; had she changed her mind so soon? Or was another noontime visitor coming to find answers for his or her broken life? I straightened in my seat and glanced over my shoulder.

"Excuse me," said a short and cheerful man who looked thirty-five. "I'm Brother Jesse." He reached out his hand to shake mine and explained, "I'm the youth minister here."

"Oh," was the only response I knew to give. I offered him my hand. "I'm a college student in the area. A sophomore. It was so warm and sunny today I decided to skip my afternoon classes and take a walk. Somehow I ended up here."

"God must have brought you," he spiritualized. "Mind if I sit down?"

How could I discourage a minister from sitting down in his own church? "Of course not," I heard myself say.

It only took a few seconds for him to slip sideways into the pew and seat himself about three feet away. "You look troubled," he observed. Was I that transparent? While I thought of an appropriate contradiction the minister proceeded, "Want to talk about it, honey?"

Honey? This man was a total stranger and he addressed me as honey? No one ever used that name anymore.

"Did the secretary tell you I was in here or something? I only came to pray, sir."

"Call me Jesse, won't you? Around here I'm just Brother Jesse," he said.

"I came in here to pray," I restated, "and that's all. I don't understand. Did I do something wrong?"

Jesse reached into the left pocket of his jacket and produced a stick of gum. "Want half?"

I nodded no.

"Most college kids that come through here during the day like this have got problems. Drugs. Pregnancies. Worse. It usually helps if they talk about it. And that's what I'm here for. Do you have a name, honey?"

"Jean," I answered.

"Just Jean?" he inquired and smiled.

"Just Jean," I echoed.

We sat quietly for a moment, but I found the silence unbearable. "This . . . this is a nice sanctuary, sir. That cross up there . . . well, it's very moving." I cleared my throat.

"I'd like to help," came his reply.

Squinting my eyes in thought, I looked into his face. Had God directed me here to Temple of Jesus to meet this man? Did Brother Jesse hold the answers to my puzzling life? If so, could I take a chance and not talk to him? Not listen?

Out came his questions. "Why don't you tell me a little about yourself, Jean? What level did you say you were at college? Do you have a major yet? Got any outside interests? Do you go to a church, honey? Ever been here? We have some real nice services for kids your age."

When I guessed he was genuinely interested I decided to follow the conversation to see where it would go. After all, if it got to be too much or too personal, I could always get up and leave. It all seemed harmless enough for now.

"No," I said, "no, I've never been here, but I'm a Christian. At least I try to be. I invited God inside a year ago February. I'm at the end of my sophomore year at school. Never thought I'd make it this far! I've been editor-in-chief of our college literary magazine this past year. I'm kind of proud of that because I'm only a sophomore. Eh . . . I guess I already told you that.

"I just got elected editor-in-chief for our next yearbook. I'll be starting my duties later on this summer and I've never headed anything that demanding before. I'm thinking I might want to be in charge of the newspaper during my senior year, who knows? It's a fact I like that kind of experience.

"I have a regular job, too," I said. "It's in a store but I hate it. I got it right out of high school and I've been there for almost two years. I don't get home until half-past eleven some nights. No other way to make it financially. I'm studying English. I don't know what else to do except try teaching, but we'll see. There," I concluded, "I think I've covered all your questions."

Jesse corrected me, "All but one."

Surprised, I looked at him and asked, "What did I forget?"

"You didn't mention what's really on your mind. Are you in trouble? There are no coincidences in God's world, honey. He brought you here to this place for a reason. I really believe it."

In my heart I wished I could be so sure of that. Perhaps my concerns would be easier to share with a total stranger. With someone I wouldn't have to see again. But how could I know for certain? I pondered awhile in silence. "You really do look worried," he observed a second time.

"You don't know what you're asking for," I cautioned. "It's all so complicated. Believe me, it is."

Jesse said nothing. He simply sat back and waited for the gush of words to come. He must have known they were on their way by the expression on my face. I knew, too.

"I don't promise to make a lot of sense," I warned.

"Go on," he urged, folding his arms.

"I'm depressed. I'm always depressed," I began. "I mean so depressed it takes all the energy I have to get up. You have no idea the courage it takes to go on day after day. I admit I was pretty scrambled up a year or so ago when I came to God. I was no prize for Him then, and I'm no prize now. But I don't know that I've changed at all. What I mean is inside. So much is the same. I just figured all the worry and hurt and bleeding would stop. But it hasn't. Far from it. It's all still here. Why is that? Do you know?"

I didn't intend to give him an opportunity to answer. Instead I plunged on. "Most of the Christians I've been around have it together, you know what I mean? They're strong. They're on top of things. But me? I always struggle. I don't care how it looks on the surface with all the activities that appear respectable, inside I feel like I'm coming apart. I always have. And I don't understand why I'm not divorced from my past if all things become new in God. You know the verses.

So do I. It's the same old story inside. Maybe when Paul was weak he became strong, but when I'm weak, *I'm weak.*

"I don't want to go through everything, but I was the most insecure kid you ever saw. There were tensions and hang-ups going back as far as I can remember in my family, and I hurt a lot. My folks split up. Thank God for that, but nothing else quite worked out. Today I live with my mother still, but my father? I haven't seen him for a few years. I hated him. As I kid I literally feared to be in the same room with him. Now I hear he's not well. That he's close to dying. I guess it doesn't really surprise me, but I still don't know how to handle the situation. After he moved out, back when I was in junior high, well, I didn't want anything to do with him. I did all I could to keep as much distance between us as possible. He'd scared me and scarred me over and over, and I wasn't going to let him keep it up. I always lost with him. Always. For me there was no such thing as winning in that family.

"My father eventually remarried but it'd take all day to fill you in on that situation, it's so complicated." I paused for a few seconds then added as an afterthought, "If my father is dying, though, I don't know what to do. I'm torn up. If I could be totally honest, I guess part of me is glad he's suffering. Part of me wants him to pay dearly for making such a miserable mess of my family and for never being a real father to me. And yet part of me wants to make up before it's too late. But how? After all this time? I can't even get into the hospital to see him because his visitors are restricted. Especially my brothers, sister, and me. It's just not an easy thing for me to cope with. Not at all. So frustrating! I feel like I'm raw with emotions that churn round and round. So many memories haunt me, sir. Too many.

"You don't mind if I go on, do you?" I inquired to be sure. I fingered through my pockets unsuccessfully for an old tissue to wipe my glasses, eyes, and face.

Jesse kindly offered me his large white cotton handkerchief and encouraged, "By all means continue. Please. You're doing fine."

It took me a moment to get situated again. "I guess you could say I'm a searcher," I continued, gazing longingly toward the large cross on the chapel wall. "I'm always looking for something to make sense inside, but nothing has so far."

Jesse stretched out a hand and touched my shoulder. I stopped. "What exactly do you mean by that, honey?" he asked. "Could you back up?"

"I mean, I thought all of this would be over when I became a Christian. That I'd have found the answer. Quote. Unquote. Good-bye struggles and hello peace of mind. I thought some lightning was supposed to zap me right into heaven on earth. That I would be removed from the old scars and all my insecurities. That I would feel good for a change. That I'd know real peace. That for once in my life I'd be . . . be . . . be *whole*." I had uttered the magic word, and tears inched over my cheeks.

"Right after I decided to become a Christian and when it dawned on me I wasn't changed, I talked it over with a couple friends my age. My best friend at the time told me I wasn't 'set free' because I didn't have the Spirit. I grew up in an old-fashioned Baptist church and I thought all I was supposed to do was invite Jesus in, but she said He wasn't enough. So Wendy and I prayed that I'd have the deeper gift of God's Spirit. But nothing happened. Then a week or two later she gave me a book on tongues and said once I had that gift, I'd have the power to resist depression. Or Satan. Or fear. You name it.

"Wendy had never talked with me like that before, and, I've got to admit, it all seemed pretty strange to me, but I was desperate. I can read pretty fast and I started reading book after book on the subject. Sometimes three or four a day if I could find the time and afford to buy them. I tell you I was desperate. Weeks passed. Wendy and I heard this great big church in town was holding a special revival, so we went. At the end of the service the speaker asked for those desiring the special gift of tongues to come forward first. I figured this was my chance. I wanted to be free and to have more of God, so I went down the aisle. I waited in a long line of people and finally the speaker put his hands on my head. Then he talked loudly, but with words I couldn't understand. Everyone expected me to faint on the floor like all the others, but I didn't. I didn't speak in another language, either. Nothing. And I walked back to my seat and out the door feeling like a real fool. A great big zero. My friend said she'd pray harder for me and maybe I should try again. But I felt stupid. Humiliated. I would never try again. Not like that. I wondered what was wrong with me. Why was I still so depressed? So unhappy? Why didn't any of this work for me?

"My devotions haven't always been the best because it's hard to go to school full time, work, be active on campus, and just try to cope. Anyway, a couple months later someone told me the key to a victorious life was having a solid devotional time each day. He said that was the answer to my problem. He was sure of it. No more emotional downs. He said God would get serious with me only when I became serious with Him. My friend also said if I fasted while I tried to draw close to God and if I prayed for changes inside that God would honor that kind of genuine sacrifice. He said I should keep it a secret, though, otherwise I'd be doing it for the wrong reasons.

"Wendy agreed with this, so I decided it was worth a try. All I wanted to do was please God and let Him know I was definitely serious. Well, I've got a real weak stomach, and I could only last about three days. The fasting made me sick. I had the dry heaves all the second day and a constant throbbing headache. I had to quit. Maybe that's why the fast didn't work. I probably didn't sacrifice enough. I don't know. I continued with the devotions, though. I guess that's something.

"A few more months passed and eventually I figured I was missing something like an inner healing, so I again sought out any and every book on the market. I reckoned that's what I needed to make me a whole person. Not a physical kind of healing from God, but an emotional release. Anything to be free. The books said all I had to do was ask God for healing, simply claim that it had been granted, and go on. I tried that. Over and over for weeks I pleaded for God to make me whole and I tried so hard to believe. But I only felt like more of a failure because I didn't have the kind of faith that pleased God. I guess He couldn't answer my prayers because my faith was so puny. I'd lost again. I fell a little deeper in despair every time I asked for His healing and was denied.

"Finally Wendy recommended a minister for me to go talk to. I wasn't so sure I trusted her judgment anymore, but I went. I poured out my story for him and he came up with two conclusions: first, there was sin in my life; and second, I needed to be anointed with oil. Apparently that's why the healing didn't occur. I've always felt guilty for being alive, so it was easy for me to confess up a storm. I do it all the time. The minister placed a drop of ointment on my head and said all I needed to do was to trust God to help me shake the depression. That it wasn't God's will that I fuss with the past. That it was even pretty disgraceful to carry emotional burdens around since God had taken care of everything at Calvary. I just had to 'let go and let God' he said. You know, take authority.

"I really thought the oil would help change me, but it didn't. At least I didn't notice anything. Again I slipped further into despair. I don't mean to be beyond God's power to reach. I don't mean to resist Him, disbelieve, or question all the time. Why couldn't there be victory for me? Huh? God must hate me for being so wishy-washy. So spineless. He must be thoroughly tired of me by now. I know I am.

"Christians are supposed to be on top of everything, right? Happy, happy, happy all the time? More than conquerors and all that? Me? I'm depressed and confused. Maybe I'm suffering from spiritual amnesia, you think? Sometimes I feel like my only alternative is to live in a mask factory: pretend I've got it together just like everyone else. I've learned I should clam up more, too, just so people will let me alone and stop judging me or assuming their answers are meant to be mine. I can't handle any more defeat. Can't people see that? Can't they see how their answers only isolate me further and further from them, from God, from hope? There are only two people I've ever known who never preached at me. There was Miss Yarger, who used to teach at the college last year. I miss her. And now there's Mrs. Logan, who's married to one of my college professors. I talk to her a lot, and she just accepts me. Eileen's gentle. She doesn't try to offer answers.

"But everyone else? Maybe they're right—maybe I'm just an inferior believer. Maybe the secret of a happy life is in confessing until I'm blue in the face, or in casting doubt and Satan aside, or in having regular devotions, or in fasting or getting anointed or claiming miracles or speaking in tongues. But I tell you I've plunged into a deeper kind of bondage this past year. Sometimes I wonder if I'm not worse off since I came to God. He's more distant than ever. I'm more of a failure than ever. I didn't always want Him but now I honestly do. The trouble is, I'm ashamed to even look up. To even admit I'm a Christian. Maybe you're headed for the Promised Land, sir, but I'm on a journey into nowhere. I figure I must be beyond God's help. I'm bound for nowhere."

I stopped to blow my nose when a half-smile spread across Jesse's face. "You think I'm funny?" I asked quietly.

"No, honey. Not at all," he responded. "You'll have to excuse me. Just this very morning I prayed that God would give me an opportunity to share this new discovery I've made in my walk with Him. I said, 'Jesus, please send someone across my path today who needs this message as much as I did!' and here you are. I told you God brought you here. I know why now."

"You do?" I said with a touch of disbelief.

"Yes. Like the word of God says, 'The shout of joy comes in the morning.' This is the morning you've been waiting for."

"It is?"

Jesse looked upward, smacked his palm on the pew in front of us, and shouted enthusiastically, "Praise you, Jesus! You never let me down!"

"He doesn't?"

"Jean, do you mind if I share with you the message that has turned my whole spiritual life around?"

I was too busy doubting to answer.

"It'll make the difference, honey. Trust me. I lived many years in darkness until God showed me the light. I can't help but want to pass it on."

What could he have discovered that was so great? Had God brought me here to listen to this man's answers? Had the morning of my life finally come? "If you think it'll help," I mumbled.

"You bet it will," he returned. "I used to be depressed a lot, too. I mean I was like a monkey swinging on some vine when it came to my Christian walk, instead of like a baby kangaroo resting in his mama's pouch." I must have looked perplexed because he asked, "You get what I'm saying?"

"I don't think so," I answered.

"Well, it's like this. Anxious people are anxious because they're always worried to death the vine won't hold 'em up. Jesus never meant us to live like that. He wants us to relax, like the little baby kangaroo trusting its mother. We don't need to cling. Don't you see? God provides!" Jesse nodded his head like this was the revelation of the century. He was by far the most energetic minister I'd met. "Right?" he asked.

"Relax because God provides," I repeated flatly.

"You're getting it, Jean. But here's the secret." From his suit jacket he whipped out a New Testament and opened it to the page with the bright red cloth marker. "In Ephesians 5:20 we read, 'Always giving thanks for all things.' There are some key words in this verse that'll get you right out of your pit of depression. The first is *always.* That means all the time. In every situation. Morning, noon, or night. *Always* is *always.* Remember that word. Next is *thanks.* We're not told to grumble or sit around feeling sorry for ourselves. No, siree. We're told to give *thanks!* But now here comes the real clincher. *For all things!* For everything! It doesn't say always give thanks for some things, or just happy things, or just the things we feel good about. God's word tells us to praise Him *for all things.* Every single thing.

"I lived so much of my life in defeat because I was so selective in what I thanked God for. One day this verse jumped off the page at me. It was like Jesus said, 'Brother Jesse, you want to know me? You want a fuller life? You got to start praising me all the time for all things I bring your way. When will you ever see they come directly from my hand? You got to start trusting me fully because I'm in charge of all things.'

"Jean, it was like the heavens opened up and I finally understood God was behind it all! Behind every little disappointment and every big heartache. Once that got through my head, it became a simple task to praise. Five years ago I would never have figured the key to happiness was so easy, but now I know. When I don't praise God it's a real insult to Him. It's like I'm saying, 'God, You really don't know what You're doing.' Only when I learn to praise Him for everything, then and only then is He free to carry His purposes to completion.

"Jean, this may seem a little harsh and I don't mean it to sting, but I really believe God is going to leave you in this mess until you learn to praise Him for everything."

I was too numb to answer.

"When things go wrong for me," Jesse explained, "God will let me stay there as long as I want to wallow around looking on the dark side. Once I say, 'Praise you, Jesus, for the furnace that went on the blink,' or, 'I don't understand it, Lord, but I praise you I'm sick today,' well, until I come to the place of total surrender in praise, God won't move me on.

"This is so important, I don't want you to miss it. As long as I choose to mope and groan about my troubles, God's hands are tied. I'm not discounting the other things you've tried before now like fasting or praying for the Spirit, but apparently God wants to teach you this lesson first. We praise Him because He's behind it all! I think you need to be very specific and say, 'Thank you, Jesus. I praise you the anointing didn't work,' or 'Praise the Lord, I'm depressed.' Only then will He work. He's waiting for you to acknowledge that His master plan for your life has no flaws. He's behind it all. Honey, have you ever tried this approach?"

A hugh sigh surfaced from deep inside and I uttered a dismayed, "No."

"It's right there in black and white in God's word. There are lots of verses that point the way to praise. 'Always giving thanks for all things!' Those six words are going to change your life, I just know it. Old Satan wants you defeated, but you just got to praise Him away. When you praise and it doesn't make sense, that's *real trust!* God can honor you then."

Jesse looked at his watch and stated, "I'm sorry, but I've got to be downtown by 2:15. Want to close in prayer?"

I hesitated a moment before answering. "I don't mind. Pray if you want."

"Okay," Jesse said. "Let's do that."

I closed my eyes and breathed deeply. If I'd had a million dollars in my pocket I'd have given it up just to erase that day. Maybe Brother Jesse was convinced he had found the world cure for all life's ailments, but his reasoning sounded like unadulterated nonsense to me.

"Father," he began, "in Jesus' name, I ask You to show Jean the truth that will set her free this very day. The more she learns to praise you for everything, the happier she'll be. And that's what she's really looking for—happiness. God, You taught me the long hard way. I praise You that You're teaching it right now to this young baby in the faith. She's going to rise up victorious this very day. Help her to know that even the worst of her days were especially planned by You for a reason. Oh, praise You. Praise You, Jesus. Praise You."

There was a long pause as I waited for his amen to know he was finished. Instead I heard him say, "Okay, Jean. Now it's your turn. Just pray what's on your heart."

Only with Wendy did I ever pray aloud. I was tired and confused and I just wanted to go home. "Dear God," I uttered. "It's me. It's Jean."

I honestly didn't know what to say. I paused a long, long time. I was sniffling once more and my eyes had filled up with the familiar liquid again. "God, I wish I knew You. Just You. I wish I could just get away from everything and everyone and meet You here. No matter how I stumble, it really is You I want to know. How could I have made such a mess of everything? God, if You could just help me through all this. If You could just see that I don't drown. I don't think I'm going to make it. I hurt, God. That's about all I've got to say now. Don't forget me, God. I need You. Amen."

I raised my head and instantly reached for the handkerchief. I felt like I was coming apart again.

"Jean?" I heard Jesse say. Why was his head still bowed? Why were his eyes still closed? "Jean?"

Not once did he look up. His eyes were sealed shut. "Jean, you missed the whole point of what I shared. I'm not going to leave until I hear you try to praise God. I know it's a little hard in the beginning, but just try it. Please. One day you'll thank me for this. Go as far back as you want and just praise God for whatever it was. Take the worst day of your childhood. The best. Go ahead. I'll wait."

I looked at the hourglass key ring beside me. I wanted to stuff it in my jeans, dart out the rear doors, and never come back. "But what if he is right?" I asked myself while I studied Jesse's bowed head. "What if all this is what I've been waiting for?"

"Dear God," I spoke aloud from the depths of my soul. "God, if this pleases You, then all right. All right, I'll try to say the words. *Thank You* for the aches that never go away. *Thank You* for all the times I hurt when I see a happy family laughing or eating or walking down the street together and I wonder why that never happened to me. *Thank You* I never knew my father," I sobbed, "and *thank You* he's close to dying and I may never get things settled."

"Yes, Jesus, yes," I heard Brother Jesse repeat under his breath. "Go ahead, Jean, you're doing fine."

Fine? I'm doing fine? I'm stripping the gears of what little emotional balance I have left, and he thinks I'm doing fine?

But I continued, "*Thank You*, God, for the childhood feelings of dread and sickness that still accompany me when I step inside a car. *Thank You*, too, for the time I ran for my life in the snow. *Thank You* the police came that day and the neighbors knew our shame. *Thank You* I've intentionally kept a distance from my brothers and sister all these years because I never wanted to hurt them again like I did that Saturday. *Thank You* for the countless times I threw up. For the nightmares that surface when I least expect them."

I broke off, hoping the panic would subside.

"Yes, Jesus, yes," Jesse prayed over and over. "Go ahead, Jean. Get it all out."

"*Thank You* I wanted to blow my damn brains all over the bedroom wall," I wept. "*Thank You* nothing's made sense and I feel like I don't belong anywhere. And *thank You* my searching's been in vain. Even today. Especially today. Nothing's made sense, but I *thank You* just the same."

For lack of anything else to say I ended abruptly with, "Amen."

I was thoroughly exhausted. I felt like I was floating in another world. Distant. In emotional shock. Physically faint. I trembled. Memories and longings meshed together into one huge, festering sore. How destructive my words seemed to me now. *Dear God, what have I done to myself?*

"Now, Jean, I want you to keep this up," Jesse urged. "Every time you get discouraged, just stop and praise God for bringing whatever it is your way. Just thanking Him in the midst of problems is not enough. No, it's thanking Him *for* them that separates the men from the boys. The winners from the losers. It works every single time, and I guarantee it'll work for you if you persist.

"And honey? If you ever want to talk or pray, you just come on back, hear? Our church is always open."

I could not find the strength to answer. I only looked with despair and hopelessness at the wooden cross before me as the hot tears continued to drop off my chin onto the clammy hands that were folded on my lap.

"I can see you need to be alone now," Jesse comforted, "so I'm going to go. Remember, God plans all things in your life and He will work them out when you exercise the praise He deserves. Don't give up. Just continue praising!"

I did not turn to look at him when he stood. The sickness in my stomach would not allow it.

"And just keep my handkerchief, honey. That's what we're here for," he assured cheerily and slipped away.

Quiet and lifeless in the empty sanctuary, I realized I had reached a new low that day. A new level of numbness and bewilderment. I knew it was impossible for me to sink any further because I had just hit bottom. I felt forsaken and betrayed by a God who not only allowed so many past hurts, but actually gave His approval. Why else praise Him for it all?

"So You were responsible, God?" I choked. "And all this time *it was You.*"

I stuffed the keys into my pocket and stood, then I walked down the aisle to the front of the sanctuary and gazed the long way up. Hanging on five metal supporters was the majestic, wooden, polished cross, the paradoxical symbol of both suffering and victory.

"So it was You?" I anguished again. *"All this time and it was You behind everything? How could You, God? How?"*

The pain was too fresh and too real for me to see the new praise gimmick for what it actually was. It would take much time, continued sorting, and more tears before I could make peace again with a God I thought had caused—not allowed, but willingly *caused*—so much to happen.

Knowing I did not belong in the cool empty chapel, I set the crumpled, wet handkerchief on the altar and vanished out into the warm April air.

12

I Never Knew You, Father

I PULLED UP the hem of my T-shirt and used it as a makeshift cleaner-
loth for my camera lens. Any professional photographer would have
ad a fit watching me swirl the cotton edge round and round the
elephoto lens, but I figured the editor of the yearbook ought to be
ble to do whatever she pleased. Besides, I was strictly amateur so
ar. That's why I was shooting roll after roll of film during the hot
ummer days of June—to get in shape for fall when college life would
esume.

I swung the camera over my shoulder and headed back to the
ouse. From a distance down the road I spotted Christine's little blue
ar in our drive. Because my mother would be working at one of the
rea hospitals until late that evening, I assumed Tina must have stopped
y to visit with Bernie and me. Plus, today was Peter's birthday;
erhaps Tina wanted all of us to take a gift or cake over to our oldest
rother's home.

"Don't move," I said and stepped over the long legs that protruded
ut from underneath Bernie's car. In one sense it was nice to have
ernie home again on his summer vacation from school, but each of
s could be a real source of irritation to the other, especially when it
ame to our constant discussions on religion. To him I was always
iberal and lost, and to me he was forever self-righteous and critical.
here was very little, if any, common ground on which to meet. We
vere clearly opposites and we learned to tolerate each other at arm's
ength only for the sake of my mother.

"Hi, Tina," I greeted and shut the side door behind me. "You
oing back out right away?" I asked when she advanced down the
arrow hallway toward me.

"Thought I'd see if Bernie would change the oil in my car while he's doing his," she answered.

"Better take something out to drink," I said. "I just heard him mumble something about iced tea when I passed by."

"I'll check," Tina replied and slipped beyond me.

I went into the living room and unfastened the camera's leather strap from around my neck. Next I went over to the stereo and put on some of my favorite albums, but not too loudly in case Bernie came in. He hated my music passionately, and he reminded me often of my worldly indulgence. I threw myself on the couch and reached down for the box of stationery I'd left much earlier that morning. It was either finish a letter or work on a research paper assigned for a summer-school course I was taking. I chose the letter.

I had barely taken the cap off my fountain pen when the telephone rang. Laziness made me wait to see if Tina or Bernie would dash in to get it, but I knew they probably couldn't hear anything from the yard. On its tenth ring I finally answered the phone and recognized my mother's voice on the other end.

"Hi," I said. "What's up?" She hardly ever called from the hospital at that time of day.

"Tina? Is that you?"

"No," I replied. "Jean. Tina dropped by and she's out with Bernie. He's probably lecturing her on the Ten Commandments right this very minute, you know him. So what's up?"

"Jean, this isn't funny," she said. "Get Tina."

"What's wrong? I questioned. "Tell me what's wrong."

"Go get your sister."

"But first I want to know what's wrong."

A sick feeling came over my stomach even before I heard her final words. "It's about your father."

She broke off and the phone line was uncomfortably still. "And? What about him?" I urged. "What is it? What have you heard? Tell me what it is."

Her voice sounded strained and broken. "He . . . he died this past weekend."

This weekend? My father? Over Father's Day? My father's dead? Why didn't anyone tell me? Why?

"And, Jean, the funeral . . ." She could not finish.

"What about the funeral?" I demanded. "Tell me about the funeral Mother."

"Jean, the funeral's over. He was buried earlier this afternoon. It's over. It's all over."

"What?" I exclaimed in shock. "What are you talking about? What do you mean the funeral's over? I don't get this at all!"

"I only just found out when I came in to work. I guess it's pretty coincidental your father was brought in to this hospital instead of one of the others in town. A couple friends in emergency came up to me a little while ago and said how sorry they were. Since I was off all weekend, they automatically assumed I knew the whole story."

"I don't believe this, Mother. This is crazy!"

"It's not crazy, Jean. I just saw a copy of the death certificate. Your father was brought in D.O.A."

My father was dead on arrival? Over Father's Day? And today's Peter's birthday? Why weren't we there? The funeral's over? What kind of a cruel joke is this? He's dead? He's buried? My father's dead? I knew he was ill, but now dead? My father's actually dead?

"Who knows why his death was kept a secret?" my mother continued calmly. "I can understand his side of the family not contacting me, but you four children had a right to know."

First keeping us from his hospital rooms and now his funeral? How cruel. How thoughtless. My father's dead? He died a mile away from my own home, and I didn't even know it? I wasn't called? D.O.A.? The funeral's over? My father's dead?

"I'll get Tina," I said, dazed.

I walked to the living room window and yelled out, "Phone. Get it, Tina. Get it *now.*" I didn't even wait for a response, but went over to the stereo, plugged in the earphones, and cranked up the volume as loud as my ears could stand the fusillade of notes. I grabbed at the stationery box and backed my way into a chair.

My father's dead. Don't think about it. Just write. Don't cry. Don't cry. You'll never stop. Write. Listen to the music. But don't think about it. Forget him. Try to forget he's dead. Forget the injustice of the years. Forget the injustice of not being with him more in the hospital or in his home or even today. Forget he's already buried. That he died without you. Forget that you never knew him. Forget this Father's Day weekend forever. Forget this is Peter's birthday. Don't cry. Don't cry, Jean. Don't start. Don't think about it. Don't let the memories return. They'll never stop. You can't handle the hurt. So just forget. Forget, Jean. Forget he's dead. Don't cry now. Don't. Don't cry. Work on your letter. Block it all out. You're almost there. Keep blocking. Fight to forget, Jean. Fight hard.

A firm hand shook and shook my shoulder. I looked up from the empty page before me and saw Tina by my side, her eyes red.

I pulled one earphone away to hear her say, "It's all over. Can you believe it? Everything's over. Even the funeral. It seems so unfair."

"I know," was the only answer I could give just yet.

"Bernie should be told," Tina suddenly remembered and looked toward the yard through the window. "And Peter, too."

I reached to fit the earphones back around my head and sighed coldly, "Yeah, don't forget Peter. Some birthday, huh?"

I couldn't bear the silence of the house any longer. Mother chose to work out the day. Tina and Bernie went to an auto store for parts to complete the half-finished tune-up. Peter was unexpectedly delayed out of town. Was it still each man for himself? Hadn't we children learned enough from the past to pull together now? And could I be dreaming all of this? Was it possible I was sound asleep? No, I was definitely awake. I knew that. But what about the tears? They would come. They were building and building from the reservoir of anger and frustration and disbelief as a hundred thoughts jumbled through my mind.

"Logan's residence," I heard at last. "This is Mike speaking."

"Hello, Mike?" I said into the telephone.

"Yeah?"

"Mike, is your mother home? This is Jean. Jean Campbell from the college."

Within a moment Eileen Logan answered, "Yes, Jean? How are you?"

She tried again, "Jean? Are you there?"

"I've been trying to reach you this last hour. I don't know who else to call, Eileen. It's my father. He's . . . he's . . . passed away. I just found out awhile ago."

"Oh, Jean. I'm so sorry," she said earnestly. "Is there anything we can do?"

"Eileen, he died over the weekend. He was buried today. I didn't find out—none of us did—until this afternoon."

"That's awful, Jean. How did something like that happen?"

"Do you think . . . could you call Carla for me? And Dr. Nichols at school? Could you ask them to pray for me? I feel so weak, Eileen. Scared."

"You know I will."

"Eileen?"
"Yes, Jean."
"Could you come?"
"You mean over to your house?"
I did not answer. I was wiping my eyes dry with the back of my hand.
"Yes, I'll be over," she said.

Eileen Logan was the most peaceful woman I had ever met. Compassionate. Loving. Warm. She was uniquely beautiful, too, in body and spirit. Eileen was genuinely interested in me from the time we'd met through her husband at college. She believed in me. In my talent. In my worth. Eileen talked and listened. She cared. Not only did she share the love of Jesus with me often, she *was* the love of Jesus to my dark, dark world. She always made me long to believe in Him, too.

There was a tapping sound at the front door, and I knew it had to be Eileen. Embarrassment and awkwardness flashed across my face. Sure, she loved me dearly, but I was ever so conscious of our differences. She had everything I lacked: a close family, a beautiful home, a profession, poise, grace, gentleness, wholeness. The list was endless.

"Come in," I greeted.
"How are you, Jean? You okay?"
I shrugged my shoulders and made a futile attempt to smile.
"I brought something for you," Eileen said and held out a small white book.
I took the thin volume from her hand and pulled away to sit on the couch. She followed. "You can read it maybe someday when you feel up to it. It's on losing our loved ones. I know the book has helped some of my friends cope, and I had an extra copy. I want you to have it."
I stared blankly at its cover before I thumbed through the opening pages. Then I thanked her.
"No one home?" Eileen asked.
I made no explanation. I only shook my head no.
"Maybe it was stupid, my asking you over and all," I apologized. "I couldn't stand the thought of being alone, but I think I'm all right now."
"I understand," she answered.
"No, I don't think you could, Eileen."
"I know this is a difficult time for you."

"That's the understatement of my life," I said. "I feel like there's an emotional storm brewing that is going to sweep me away any second. I can't explain it. One minute I feel absolutely numb and the next I feel every conceivable emotion. There's all sorts of confusion. Hurt. Anger."

Eileen clutched her hands around mine. "Jean? Try to remember the good times with your father. Remember those times and let them carry you through this."

"Good times?" I stated flatly. "Good times? You don't know what you're saying, Eileen. You don't know the full story. Believe me, there's so much I've never told you. There's a lot I've never told anyone.

"You think you know me, Eileen. You've read through all my poetry. You've listened to me go on and on about God and what a mystery His love is to me. You've heard me criticize the college to death and talk about current politics. And you know some sketchy facts about my family and that I'm forever unhappy. But I've never let you in—totally inside—all the mess. I figured you couldn't understand. I figured you wouldn't want anything to do with me if I told you how mixed up I really was. How depressed. How weak. How angry. How much I want to quit living."

Eileen's eyes watered up. "I know I love you, Jean. I know God loves you."

"But you've never walked in my shoes," I explained. "I would never wish that on anyone."

"You are special," she returned. "You have worth and I love you."

"You don't understand who I really am. You'd reject me."

"I know I love you," she repeated tenderly, squeezing my hand hard. "I know you have worth. Nothing will ever change that. Trust me."

We grew very quiet. Eventually I stuttered, "Eileen . . . not . . . not many people know this . . . but . . . but I made it in to see my father a few weeks ago."

"You did?" she asked with surprise.

"Not at the main hospitals in town, but at another one he was transferred to. I think the doctors had done pretty much all they could do, and I got in right before he was released from there to rest finally at home."

"But how, Jean?" Eileen questioned. "How did you manage that when you'd failed a number of times to see him before?"

I paused to think. "I kept calling his hospital floor a couple times a day for his condition. One night a nurse said she'd have to check on him first to be sure how he was doing. She offered to call me back and for some reason—I don't even know why—I mentioned I was a college student. She asked me where, and when I told her she got very interested and said that's where her husband taught."

"Who?" Eileen wondered.

"It was Dr. Tressler's wife. Luckily I'd had straight *A*'s when I had Tressler for class, and I knew that would somehow help me. She would take me seriously. I tried to explain that my father was dying, and that I wanted to see him but couldn't."

I stopped talking long enough to recruit the inner strength to continue my story. "And it had to be God, that's all I can say. Within the week Mrs. Tressler gave me a map of his hospital floor. No joke, Eileen. She did. She told me when to visit and how to enter unnoticed. She said she and some of the other nurses felt my father needed to see me as much as I needed to see him. That he was alone nearly all the time. That he was weak. Very lonely. Very ill. Well, I knew I had to go. I knew I might never get the chance again. But what do you say to a man you never knew? A man you were always so afraid of? What if he turned out to be just as bitter and angry as I last remembered him? Then what?

"I know this sounds strange, Eileen, but I took along my camera. I never thought of taking his picture but I wish now I had." I pointed to the silver-black lens case that rested on the living room desk and continued, "I took it because he was always interested in photography. That was about the only positive thing I could remember about him from my childhood. He sometimes used to shoot for weddings and things like that when I was real young.

"I've never told anyone this before, but the biggest reason I wasn't so keen on accepting responsibility for the yearbook at college was because whenever I saw camera equipment I was reminded of my father. That's the honest truth, Eileen. And I wasn't ready yet to touch anything that brought him to mind. Still, when the opportunity opened for me to be editor, I somehow convinced myself to try, regardless.

"I took my camera that day because I figured he might be proud that his daughter grew up into somebody halfway responsible. Maybe he'd be proud of me for following his love for photography, I didn't know. I was grabbing at straws. I also figured if things got to be too awkward I'd ask for his advice on how to shoot candids or group pictures. I needed something to fall back on.

"Mrs. Tressler's instructions were perfect down to the last letter. I prayed earnestly that God would get me in and out of that hospital without any problems. That He'd give me the courage to speak up and to look my father straight in the eye. That I would say the things I needed to say while there was still time.

"Mrs. Tressler tried her best to prepare me. She said my father was pretty frail, but it was still a shock when I saw him face to face. He used to be a strong, muscular man, Eileen. Real strong. But by then he couldn't even sit up in bed. His legs were pencil thin. I'll never forget the way he looked. I tell you, he wasn't the father I remembered. Not at all.

"He recognized me as soon as I walked in. His face even lit up. That surprised me. Since he'd had a stroke a number of months ago on top of everything else, well, he could barely talk above a whisper. A nurse brought me a very high stool and I put it directly beside his bed. I couldn't believe I was actually there. That people were helping me at last, even though it was clearly against their previous orders.

"It's hard to remember everything we talked about. There was no bitterness, Eileen. My father was much too sick for that. I told him about college and that I was proud to be going on my own. Working my way through, I mean. I told him about the writing I'd done. Some awards. About being editor-in-chief of the college literary magazine and now the yearbook. He tried to smile when I told him about the photography I'd have to learn. His eyes got real red when I showed him the camera, but he was too weak to take it out of my hands. I thought he was going to cry. He was awfully tired.

"I never remember my father philosophizing. Not ever. I think now maybe he was too ashamed to try with only his tenth grade education behind him. He was full of philosophy that day, Eileen. He talked about life mostly, and how spring *always* followed winter. He talked about the last few years. How sick he'd been. How unhappy. How drained.

"I told him I'd heard that he didn't ever want to see any of us again. That Peter and Tina and Bernie and I had heard he was through with us. That he thought we were only after his money or something strange like that. I told him we'd all tried and tried to get into the hospitals to see him, but there was always the restriction on his room that he wasn't supposed to have visitors. I asked him pointblank, 'Father, do you hate us now? Do you hate me? Do you want us to stay away?'

"His head turned slowly back and forth on his pillow and he whispered, 'No. No. No. No. But it's too late now. It's all come too late.' And I could tell he was choked up.

"He was getting drowsy. I'd kept him awake almost an hour, telling him all about my brothers and sister and me. I knew it was time to go. I got off the stool and leaned directly over the bed. 'Father,' I said to him. 'Father, all my life I've been afraid and confused. I don't know what it's like not to hurt, but I'm sorry. I'm sorry for anything I did against you back then and all the years since. *Forgive me.*'

"He nodded his head a little and closed his eyes. With all my heart I wanted him to say the words back to me, 'Forgive me, too, Jean,' but he didn't. I waited and waited. He was fighting to stay alert but he was losing. I prayed frantically that God would help him say the words. They never came, Eileen. He could barely open his eyes every other minute to see if I was still there.

"It wasn't long before sleep had won. I remember everything vividly, even how the room seemed to get darker. Darker than ever. I remember I kissed his forehead and wiped off the tears that had splashed from my face onto his. I prayed for him there and then got to sobbing hard. He never did wake up, Eileen. Eventually I gathered my purse and camera and then touched his face for the last time. The very last time. The last time ever. I felt my heart surely must be tearing into a thousand pieces. It was a much different kind of pain than I'd ever felt before.

"I walked across the room and took one final look around. I remember leaning my head against his door to bid him farewell. I know he couldn't hear me, but I talked to him like he could. I remember I asked him, 'Why? Why did it have to be this way, Father? Why then? Why now? Why has it all come to this? I guess I'll never understand. Do you? Is this good-bye? But I never knew you, Father. I guess you never knew me either. Yet, like you said, it *is* too late now. Father, *if I don't see you again,* please know my thoughts are always with you. How I wish it could have been different all along for each of us. For you. For me. Good-bye, Father. It's time to go. Good-bye.'

"I left that room, Eileen, and that was the last time I ever saw him. I can't explain it, but somehow deep inside my heart I knew we would never meet again. At least not in this lifetime. As I look back now, I suppose that was perhaps the holiest, the finest hour we had ever spent together. I . . . I should let Mrs. Tressler know. I should let her know he's gone. I should thank her again for putting her job on the line like that and helping me. I should thank her for her prayers. For giving me that hour with him. I'll never be able to pay her back."

Not all friends can sit alone in silence comfortably, but then, not everyone is blessed with the gentle love of Eileen Logan. If anyone could penetrate my pain, I was sure it was Eileen. I could tell it in her eyes as we thought quietly together side by side. I could also tell that this precious woman would continue to reassure me of her love and God's through the months and perhaps years of searching ahead. I knew I was not alone, and I drew much strength from the inner witness of that fact when I looked into her face.

"Eileen, I think I'll be okay now by myself," I said. "And the others will be coming home soon. I just want to go to bed right now. Maybe think awhile more. Sleep if I can."

She spoke softly, "Sure, Jean."

We both stood and looked at each other, then sighed heavily.

"If there's anything I can do, you just call, Jean. Promise? Bill and I care. Others at the college care, too. I'll be in touch, but you call or come over anytime."

"Thanks, Eileen," I said under my breath. "You're the best."

"God loves you," she comforted. "He hasn't abandoned you. Don't forget that."

"Eileen? Eileen, before you go can I ask you something?"

"Yes, Jean. What is it?"

"Do you think . . . Eileen, could you hug me? Just hug me, that's all."

"Of course," she agreed and quickly took the step between us.

For what seemed like an eternity, the healing touch of her stronger arms around mine dispelled the darkness of that awful day. She gave me strength for the long night ahead. Courage for the days to come. Of all the gifts Eileen had ever given me, of all the gifts yet to come from her hand, I could never treasure any above that solitary embrace. It was the first time in my life I had *ever* experienced the loving arms of Jesus enfold me tightly.

"I love you, Jean," I heard her say.

"I love you too, Eileen," I said and hugged harder.

From the front room window I watched Eileen get into her car and pull out the drive. "Oh, God," I wept in the empty house. "I need her more than ever now. And I need *You* more than ever. Don't let me drown in this storm, Lord. Keep me in one piece. Please, Jesus. Please. I'm so scared. Don't leave me now, God. Don't ever leave me. Amen."

13

The Farewell

Good Friday
5:17 A.M.

Dear Father,

It's now been well over three years since your death, so I'm not exactly sure how to do this. I'm not even sure you'll get my letter, but I have prayed that God would both help me write this and help me relinquish this into His hands. If it's at all possible, He will speed it on to you. I must believe that.

Remember when I was a little girl and afraid of the dark? It was only because I thought ghosts lurked over and under the bed. Once the light was on I could see how silly my fears were. But you, Father, you have been a different kind of ghost for me. You are ever present. Ever real. Ever fearful. No matter how I grope and grope for the switch to dispel you, you are always there in my memory. You are always there to overshadow today. I wonder how I can expose you to the light, Father. I wonder how I can free myself from your influence once and for all.

Do you know something? Just about every day of my life I've felt like a failure because of you. I never once remember your praise. Under your roof I felt worthless as a child. Confused. Inadequate. Unwanted. In the way. Helpless and without much hope. I felt like I was terribly, terribly weak then. Even crazy. Inferior to anyone and everyone. And Father? I feel all of these emotions today. They are still with me *today*.

Sometimes Mother contributed to my sense of worthlessness as I grew up, or brothers or sister unknowingly. But basically it was you

I learned to blame for all the years of insensitivities and injustices. It was you I learned to hate. It was you I knew to avoid. I doubt if you could fathom the fear I had for you, Father. Not just before the divorce, but ever since.

During the years after your death I have prayed and wept, searched and wept, and agonized and wept. Only recently have I been able to ask God to turn my fear and hatred of you into something less destructive for me. *I want to get well and I want to move on.* I may never come to love you in any tender or sentimental way, I may never embrace my childhood years with fond recollection and wish them back, but I am open this Good Friday morning to understand your callousness. With God's help this morning I will try to see the hurting child in you.

The fact that you never finished school has provided a lot of insight for me. As a beginning English teacher, knowing what I do about high school dropouts, I wonder if you didn't feel worthless most of your life because of your unfinished education. Did you quit because you felt inferior intellectually to most others at school? Was that it or something else entirely? And have you felt like a loser since? Less educated? Inarticulate? Unrecognized?

Father, not long ago I heard another important fact about your upbringing that's helped me put a large piece of your puzzle in place. I've learned that you ran far away from home as a teenage boy. I had thought of running away a number of times myself, *but you actually did it. You ran.* You also must have been lacking love and support at home. How ironic, Father. How ironic that our frustrations were so much alike, when for years both you and I were strangers in the same household.

So you quit school. You ran away. You worked at odd jobs before you met and married Mother. Then you lived happily for a while, though poor. You had children. Peter first. Christine. Bernie. And then, about the time you were in and out of employment, you had me. I remember nothing of those lean years of financial strain, but I can guess that you must have been pressed to the limit trying to cope with the regular daily needs of a growing family as well as Tina's and Bernie's recurring illnesses. Any man would have been. How *did* you cope without hospitalization or unemployment benefits to help ease the burdens? Were the seams of your life just beginning to tear back then? At about the time I arrived?

I've also pondered your disillusionment in God. You were a deacon. You were an elder in a local church before I was born. Then, quite suddenly, you pulled away because of a bitter disagreement with a pastor friend. No one seems to know what that debate was all about for sure, but it must have burned like acid for you to have lost faith in everything and everybody. Was this another seam that burst wide open? Was this the seam that gave way to all the others?

I honestly do not know if you turned to alcohol because your marriage was deteriorating, or if the marriage was deteriorating because you turned to alcohol. (I suspect the latter.) No matter how awful it was without work, or how high the doctor and hospital bills rose, or what fine Christian example let you down, *alcohol was not the answer.* Alcohol was the easy way out for you, Father, but it was the hard way out for the rest of us. How can I ever forgive you for taking the path of avoidance? Of destruction? Did you think you were less responsible for your actions if you drank? Did you think the rest of us were untouched and unaffected by your drinking?

Nearly all of my vivid memories of you were those when you drank or when you argued irrationally. That was about the only legacy you left me, Father. I felt cheated. Insane with anger at you especially, but also with God and anyone else. I wanted to be loved. I wanted to be special. *I wanted a home.* Peter, Christine, and Bernie at least remember you before your years of rebellion and anger, but I never knew you that way, Father. It occurs to me now that I never knew you at all.

Recently I dug through old picture albums trying to find photographs of you and me together. No luck. I pulled at childhood memories, longing to recall times in your arms or the sound of your laughter. No luck again. I asked Mother if she could remember gifts or toys you gave me, but she couldn't. Her eyes swelled up with tears, though, and she shared a tender moment from her remembrance of you. She told me of the time just weeks before I was born. Peter, Bernie, and Tina were playing on the couch together one evening. She said you studied them for a long time then you whispered to her, "Three children are fine, but the fourth will make it *perfect.*" I was a part of your dream? I would complete the family circle? Father, what went wrong? Why did I never know your tenderness? Your love? Why did I never know you?

This Good Friday sunrise while I sit quietly in bed, reflect, and write to you, I find I'm too fatigued to sort through each of the old perplexities and bring them up one by one. Besides, it is physically impossible to unscramble scrambled eggs. Herein is the truth I've found: for all my desire, I cannot change the past. I cannot come a second time from Mother's womb and try again, this time with everyone waiting on stage to pick up their cues correctly. No, the die is cast. The damage is done. There is no turning back. There are only miles of unfinished roads ahead for me, and I fear the way is rough. More sifting and searching. More building and rebuilding. The path you left for me is lonely, Father. It is exceedingly hard. Exhaustive.

The sun is finally coming up outside my bedroom window as old scattered images from the past replay once more in my mind. But today, how do I pull all these fragmented thoughts together and finally make peace with you? I am ragged from the weight of your influence, Father. I am weary from shadowboxing little Jeanie's images of a towering, gruff father—a father who is gone and who I now know was a weak man underneath his angry disguise. A man full of flaws. A struggler. But now he is gone. You are gone, Father.

I do not know what to do with this bitterness I feel toward you, but to commit it into God's hands before it consumes me. All the hatred, too. I cannot nurture either of these another day and still long for wholeness, because bitterness, hatred, and wholeness cannot and will not exist together. It has taken me four painfully long years to learn that truth. Today I choose to take one giant step along the path of healing.

Father, may God consecrate these words and tears this morning. May I not be uttering hollow desires only to discover in time the issue of forgiving you is still unsettled. I want to forgive you. Not tomorrow. Not next year. But now. Today. I want to give up the resentment and move on. God help me to do just that today. I am willing today. I am open today. I am ready today.

What is there left to say, Father? Please hear me now: *wherever you are, think kindly of me, forgive me, and if it's possible after all these years, even love me. And with the help of my heavenly Father, I will do the same for you.*

It is finished.
The shadowy spell is broken.
Farewell, Father. Farewell at last.

Jean

14

Arena

WHY DON'T YOU *begin by telling me how you decided on me as a counselor and what you think I can do for you, Jean. By the way, would you like some coffee?*

No. No thanks.

Tea?

I guess so. Sure.

Just help yourself, but I think I ran out of sweetener this morning. Will it matter?

Not at all. I like tea better without sugar. Maybe a little honey sometimes, but no sugar.

Here. Set it on this. It's probably too hot to hold.

Ouch! You're right.

It seems we only get two water temperatures with that heating unit: lukewarm or steaming.

Well, it's definitely set on super hot today. I'll give it some time to cool.

Are you comfortable? Or would you like to try that chair?

I'm fine here. You know, I feel like I'm in a living room instead of an office.

I was never one for desks and straight-back chairs. I prefer the atmosphere of home furnishings much better. I think everybody feels more relaxed that way.

I like it. It's less intimidating. For me it is.

That's good to hear. Jean, now that we're both settled, you won't mind if I take notes, will you?

No.

I'd like to get back to my initial question, if I may. How did you make the decision to come to me?

Well, I chose you because you are a psychologist who is also a Christian. I figured you would understand me better, Dr. Andrews, since a lot of my struggles tie in directly with my faith in God. You asked me why I've come. I guess I'm here because progress seems terribly slow while I hack away at personal issues all by myself. I'm hoping you can short-circuit time. In the last year or two I've worked through some major hurdles, especially where my father is concerned, but I've got miles and miles to go. I figure it'll help if I talk things out.

Just after my father died I'd sometimes go and talk with a minister at a church near the college. He's a Quaker man. Very gentle. Accepting. Caring. I've never met any other man quite like Pastor Jim. If I was ever curious what Jesus must be like, I only had to look to Jim's life and the interest he took in me. I think I owe my sanity to him. Seriously, I do. He pulled me through some mighty troubled waters. He's not there now, but when I talked with him I always felt better. Then there's Eileen Logan. She's married to one of the college professors where I went to school. I don't know what I'd have done without both of these people. They helped me most by listening, I guess. By withholding critical judgment. By genuinely caring. I've come here today hoping you will do the same with me.

I've got to be honest, though, and tell you I'm not one hundred percent comfortable about seeing a clinical psychologist. In a lot of Christian circles it's a sign of distrusting God. You know, like I've given up on God's ability to answer or heal or whatever by turning to you. I'm kind of ashamed to be here. I know a lot of people will be very speculative and read it as a sign of failure for me. They'll figure I've flopped in managing my own life and that I must be a basket case or something.

But you came despite what people might say.

Yes.

Why?

Why? Scripture says we shouldn't walk in the counsel of the ungodly, so I'm not. I want a Christian counselor. Someone with a Ph.D.—that's important to me—and someone I can trust. I admit I don't want to make a lifetime career out of seeing you, but it helps just to know you're available. As far as what other people might say, they don't know how desperate I feel. They don't understand the anxiety I carry around or the insecurities that still plague me. Maybe if these people were in my shoes and had walked where I've walked they'd have come much sooner. Probably. I bet so.

I'm familiar with the old stereotypes. It's sad that more people in today's churches aren't sensitive to the complexities of human problems. But the trend is changing.

I hope you're right.

Jean, how, specifically, do you think I can help you? Let's define it. What would you like from me?

Like I said, I guess I'd like you to let me talk. Based on your expertise I'd like you to tell me if there's hope for me. Will I ever be whole? Really whole? Is there a way we can cooperate with God to relieve the pain of my shattered past, to restore the broken image inside me? Or is it totally up to God as to how He refashions and when? Even if He chooses to wait until eternity? I think you could help me by letting me wrestle aloud with my faith. And I'd like you to sort through other past and present struggles with me to put them in a new light. I know there must be a dozen issues I could work on, but I think I'd like to tackle my self-image first. It's a big one.

Self-image?

Yes.

Tell me why you want to begin there.

I guess because every single day when I look in the mirror I see someone I really don't like at all. I see a little, cowering girl in a grown-up body. Even though she's known several levels of success, when it comes right down to it, she's rarely content. And generally she doesn't like who she sees in the mirror. Sometimes she hates who she is.

Why is that? Why would you hate yourself? Can you put it into words for me?

I don't know exactly. I'm very critical of everything I do. I discount most of it and rarely give myself a break. Others, yes. Me, no. I know it's a double standard, but ever since I can remember I've felt like a zero. A waste. When I was a kid at church I picked up the idea that any preoccupation with self was pride, and pride was one of the seven deadly sins. It was okay to criticize ourselves to death, but to praise or think kindly of ourselves? Never.

I think my home life contributed to my insecurities more than anything else, and I suspect many insecurities were bred into me long before my parents' divorce. I don't know if I lived with a lot of criticism or what, but I was anxious all the time. And I do mean all the time. For about a year while my folks were getting their divorce I went to a counselor off and on because I was coming apart. Somewhere I got the idea it was my fault I wasn't tougher. I started blaming myself for being so weak, and I've been blaming myself ever since.

And?

And I get depressed. When I'm down I honestly believe other people—no matter who they are or what they've done—I believe other people always matter and I don't. Others count in this life and I do not. Others are redeemable, but I'm beyond help. Again, I can see it's a double standard, but I don't know how to break free. It's almost like a homing instinct inside me that says I need to be punished for being inadequate, inferior, and anxious. Or that I'm doomed to lose in life and that I deserve to lose.

Let's back up a minute. You mentioned self-interest tying in with pride. I don't see them as the same thing at all. I'm curious what you do with verses in the Bible that speak of loving our neighbors as ourselves? Or the reality that Jesus died for us? Sinners, yes. All of us. But sinners who must have had worth in His eyes.

The problem is not that I don't see worth in others, Dr. Andrews. The problem is that I don't see worth in me. It's not so much in forgiving others, but in forgiving myself and in acknowledging I am worth forgiving. It's not in accepting others, but in accepting myself and in seeing I am worth accepting. I know the verses. I can rattle them off in two or three minutes. I don't have any qualms in looking at another human being and seeing his or her uniqueness. I do believe that other people are special. Really I do. But to turn those verses around to include me? It's like old voices or tapes from the past choke out anything of worth and value in me. Or it's like a machine readout inside me that says, "Does not compute . . . does not compute . . . reject." I see myself as the exception to whatever rule of love or grace or worth God has for His children. Am I making any sense?

Tell me about the old tapes or old voices from the past. If we could make them talk out loud, what would they say about you?

Let me think a minute. If I'm going to be utterly transparent, I imagine they would say, "Jean Marie Campbell, you are a poor excuse for a human being. You don't handle stress well. You've screwed up your life. You shouldn't have let anything get to you as a kid or all the years since. So you're a Christian now, eh? Big deal. If you're a Christian, then why don't you act like one? You're supposed to be on top of things. Content like everyone else. A regular Rock of Gibraltar.

Never worried. Never depressed. Never angry. Always up, up, up. Always sugar-coated and whistling a happy tune through life. Always trusting and fearless. You try hard, but why don't you just face facts and admit that if you haven't gotten your act together by now, kid, you never will?"

How often do you say these things to yourself, Jean?

I can't put a number to it, if that's what you want. It's kind of an unspoken belief I've just accepted. I know I don't need anyone else to harass and degrade me. I'm aware that I'm doing a terrific job of that myself. But the question is, how do I stop the vicious cycle? I don't think I would ever talk to anyone else the way I talk to myself. Like a snake with its venom, I'm the one responsible for pumping old poisons into my own system. I know I'm doing it and I know it's destructive, but how do I finally stop? How do I change? How will I ever recognize my worth and stop tearing myself down?

Of course, we'll need to go into this more thoroughly later. But to respond to your questions briefly, let me say it's going to take a lot of hard work on your part and a lot of inner discipline to replace the old negativism. I think the answers rest in your ability to challenge the old voices. Test them out. See if they're appropriate for Jean Campbell's life today. Look logically at your past performances and string of successes—you've been through college; you've been honored to receive the student's favorite teacher vote for several years in a row; you've been published in some magazines and anthologies; and you're even in the process of writing a book about your teaching experiences, a book that's already been accepted for publication—and ask yourself if the old tapes were justified. And more importantly for you now, I think you need to ask yourself if the voices are appropriate today. Before you can begin to challenge the voices effectively, however, you need to identify them and to acknowledge just where they originated.

I read through your written personal assessment survey before you came in this afternoon, and I can already see many strong, predictable connections between your childhood experiences and how you see yourself now. For example, one of the things you wrote in your biographical statement that intrigued me was the image of the tree. Do you remember how you worded that?

I think I said I felt like I was over a huge canyon as a kid, hundreds of feet up, with only a limb to hang onto. And all I could do to survive was cling tightly and shut my eyes. Something like that.

Right. And you went on to write that even as an adult you have the sensation of clutching that limb. You wrote that you are overwhelmed because you have so far to go in order to land.

But that's how it feels inside, Doctor. I'm not exaggerating. I still feel like I'm hanging way up there.

But based on your outward performance and how you've learned to cope, I think there's a lot you can challenge, Jean.

I don't follow.

You felt abandoned, panicky, and desperate as a girl holding onto the tree limb. You feel the same today. But the truth is, if you would open your eyes and look down, you would no longer see hundreds of feet of air between you and the ground. Probably only a few inches are left. Even if you did "bottom out" and fall, you don't have far to go. You're clutching and afraid when only a few inches are left. Challenging the voices that tell you you're hundreds of feet up might be a place to begin to help you relax. The voices are powerful, I realize, but they're also very deceiving. They keep you twisted in knots. Do you follow?

I'm not sure.

Let me back up. When we begin to expose a lot of the inner "self-talk" you churn around in your thoughts, I think you'll be able to see that many of the ideas and concepts you developed as a child are irrational. Children do not have many reasoning skills. They basically receive whatever's happening to them and react on impulse. All kids do that. You did. And Jean? It was okay for you to be a vulnerable girl then. With what resources you had, you hung on. You've come through it all. You could have run away, or become self-destructive and so forth, but you came through it. You made some wise choices and you managed to stay afloat. A lot of others haven't.

Now that you're a maturing adult, it's time for you to challenge the old voices. And it's good if we begin with basics like your worth and self-love. I want you to know you won't change overnight, but, yes, with a lot of hard work you can shed many of the thinking patterns you've already established. Not all of the thinking patterns, but many. Realistically, you'll be working on some for life, and it won't be easy. I'd like to promise you it will be but I can't. I need to emphasize in this first session that you will hear no pat answers from me. Not the way I interpret psychology or theology.

I know, Dr. Andrews. I know.

If I've developed an appreciation for anything in my years as a psychologist, it's that people are highly intricate. No two people are alike, ever. No set of circumstances will ever be reproduced exactly. That's just the way it is. And I've especially observed this in matters pertaining to faith. The Christian experience is a lot more intricate than we give it credit for. A lot more.

I'd heard that philosophy about your counseling before I came. To be honest, it's what finally drew me to you. I don't try to make my life complicated, Doctor, but it seems that way to me. And do you know something? You've zeroed in on one of my own touchy spots. I've already discovered plenty of secular books on the market and secular speakers out there who relay pop psychology to the masses. I've also come to the conclusion we have people in evangelical circles who similarly promote what I call pop religion. The school of easy believism. Polyester Christianity complete with pat answers. Spiritual pep talks and effervescent songs and books that offer candy-bar highs in place of sound nutrition.

In a culture that breeds instant everything, I understand why people want quick solutions, but I've got to tell you I'm skeptical through and through. When I look back at all the sorting and reading and listening I've done since I became a Christian, I sometimes feel like I've been sold a hollow bill of goods, and primarily by the influences of pop religion. Is life so simple that it can be defined in one, two, three easy steps? Are we that simple? Is God? Or Satan? The problem of evil? Or pain? Suffering? Sin? *No. A thousand times no.*

I can't speak for anyone else, but I've reached my saturation point. No more fluffy, enchanting formulas on how to live the Christian life or how to conquer this or that. No more cookie-cutter claims that are supposed to fit all of us at the same time in exactly the same way. No more. I can't handle pop religion, Doctor, and I can't handle all the hype and commercialization that goes with it. It's not for me. Instead I want depth and scholarship. I want substance. Authenticity. I want to know, to actually strip away all the sugary, superficial hindrances and to *know* the reality of God that can reach and touch me where I live and breathe and hurt.

Dr. Andrews, I can't see much good coming from my background yet, but I sometimes wonder if I won't emerge through all these spiritual and emotional struggles to become wiser. Stronger maybe. Deeper. More fulfilled than if I weren't so sensitive and inquisitive. I wonder if, in the years to come, I won't develop an unshakable faith for all the painful searching. I hope so. How I hope so. Beyond all the questions and confusion in my life, it really is God I want to know and follow. It is. I want wholeness, but not apart from God. What am I saying? God *is* wholeness.

Do you have any Kleenex in here?

Sure, Jean

Thanks.

You look very reflective. What were you thinking just then when you stopped?

If I could discover more of God. More of completeness. Do you know what it's like being suspended in mid-air for a lifetime? Do you know how worn I feel? How overwhelmed when I think that after all the tears and years and work behind me, there are more tears to be shed and more years and work ahead? Sure, now I'm a Christian and my life's redirected, but that doesn't mean I don't want to quit sometimes. Why does growing up take so long?

We are all in the process of growing up.

I hear you, but I'd like to get out of the first grade, if you know what I mean.

Perhaps life is a school. I don't know that any of us ever fully and completely "arrives." I think we're always stretching to grow, at least those of us who don't want to stagnate.

I tell my students that. I tell them to stretch. To aim high. Not to give up. Still it's a lot easier to say than to accept.

True. Very true.

This is a little off the track, but as much as I get scared for me and whether I'll last to sort out all my hang-ups, I really get scared when I look into the faces of my kids at school. If it's been an uphill fight for me all my life, how much more of a struggle do they face? Kids who've been raped? Abandoned? Young teens with criminal records already? Runaways? Those battling alcoholism or drug addiction? What's ahead for them? I tell you I get numb when I imagine them ten or twenty years down the road. Life for me hasn't been any picnic, but those kids? Life is already hell. Apart from God, what hope is there for them to undo the damage? I wonder how they ever will face their futures and make it.

Teaching's been very good for you, hasn't it?

For now I feel at home there. I don't understand the dynamics of everything, but I come alive with kids in a special way. I care for them. I hurt with them. Teaching's helped me mature. It's helped me learn how to reach out to teens who remind me so much of myself, especially in the way they cope with family conflicts and divorce. The number of kids who've experienced brokenness is *staggering* to me. God help them. Can you imagine what it will be like in our country's future if we ever have a whole nation of adult kids who've suffered the wounds of divorce? Or alcoholism? Just because they'll age physically is no sign they'll age emotionally. Hardly. We have a lot of adult bodies walking around right now with hurting, shattered children inside who long for love. I ought to know. I'm one of them.

Maybe you don't fully realize it yet, Jean, but there are a lot of people who envy the very strengths you take for granted. You're intelligent and you're creative. It's time we start to turn that around for you. To let you relax and feel good about yourself. To repair some of what's been shattered.

Anything new scares me, but with God's help I think I'm ready. Now, more than ever before, I know it's time for a new beginning. And I'm ready, Dr. Andrews. I'm finally ready.

15

Two Winds

EILEEN LOGAN PUSHED her breakfast plate away, touched the blue napkin to her lips a final time and furrowed her eyebrows together in amazement. "How many miles did you say, Jean?"

"Thirty," I answered. "Thirty on the nose."

"Thirty?"

"Yes, Eileen. Thirty miles."

"You rode thirty miles yesterday on your ten-speed?"

"It's no big deal," I replied. "You know I try to do five or ten miles a day as it is. Yesterday I just happened to do thirty. It beats jogging."

"But thirty miles?"

"Eileen, my goal is to do a few fifty-mile stretches before summer's up—maybe even a hundred in one day—so thirty's nothing."

"I still can't figure it," she teased. "Thirty miles and you're up walking around so well today?"

I exaggerated a loud sigh then grinned. "Will you stop with the jokes already? I'm trying to be serious here. I went out so I'd have some time to reflect, that's all."

"Honestly, Jean. After the first mile I'd be too exhausted to think!"

"Eileen."

Her voice calmed as she answered, "All right. I'll settle now. Back to your biking story. Go ahead. I'm listening."

"For sure?" I asked.

"Trust me," she stated. "Go on."

I pulled my chair closer to the table and began, "Well, I get a lot of insight when I go out riding. Besides, with the excitement over my dedication party this afternoon to celebrate the release of *Reaching Out With Love,* I just wanted to be alone and think. There's so much to sort through, you know? Not just with my very first book coming out either, but I found lots of other things to ponder while I chalked up the miles."

Eileen whisked a delicate strand of hair from her forehead and asked, "Like what, for instance?"

I clutched the small orange glass in front of my plate and downed the last of my breakfast juice. "A thousand things, Eileen. At least a thousand. For one—and I know this sounds crazy—for some reason yesterday I happened to remember a favorite book I had when I was a kid back in the seventh grade called *The Scarlet Letter*. It's an old classic. Surely you've read it, haven't you?" I reached across the wooden table and playfully tapped my friend's shoulder. "That is, if you think you can remember that far back."

"Oh, very funny," she laughed good-naturedly. "Now who's making the jokes?"

"Joking?" I questioned. "Joking? Was I joking?" I said and waited for her humorous scowl. Folding my arms against the edge of the table, I grew serious. "Enough. I'll quit. But have you read *The Scarlet Letter?"*

Eileen peered through her kitchen window to the back yard while I studied the graceful curve of her face. "I think so," she replied, "but it's been a while. Isn't it about a woman who has an illegitimate child and doesn't own up to the father's identity? Set back in the early days of New England? By Nathaniel somebody?"

"Hawthorne," I completed. "Nathaniel Hawthorne. That's the book."

Eileen Logan's countenance always seemed to glow when she smiled, and it was illumined now. "See there?" she mused. "I'm not as rusty as you think."

"Perish forbid!" I returned quickly.

Within seconds came her question, "So why'd you think of that book after all this time?"

I propped one hand underneath my chin as a headrest to help me think. "I don't know exactly, but I was always so intrigued with the character of Hester Pryne when I first read the book. Remember her punishment? For her entire life she had to wear the scarlet letter *A*, an ugly symbol for adultery, but something which she immediately turned into a beautiful piece of embroidery. It never dawned on me until yesterday that we are alike, Hester and I. We're both highly creative and sensitive individuals. We've both felt burdened by a lot of personal shame. We each resisted the desire to run away. We've been greatly misunderstood by the people around us, and we compensated by burying our hidden secrets deeper for a time. We've felt alone in the world. We both felt desperate for love. We've both managed to survive.

"Pain and all, Hester wore that letter *A* each day of her life. What hit me with such force yesterday was that people eventually forgot what the scarlet letter represented. By the end of the book, townspeople were literally convinced the *A* stood for *Ability,* not adultery. They revered her. She went from total disgrace to genuine victory. From the community scaffold to triumph and usefulness. Can you believe it? Always both strong and fragile, always both afraid and courageous, Hester became the envy of most people in town. That fact astounded me.

"Eileen? God knows I'd have wished for some changes in my own upbringing to have promoted a healthier child product. I confess I don't have a lot of answers today to offer people, and I am light-years away from earning my own *A* in Ability, but I am charting my course in that direction. I pray I am. Like Hester, I know my life must somehow be purged in depth because of my past struggles. I don't like the road I have traveled, the bitter tears I have wept, and all the years I wasted blaming God for scars He did not create, but I have learned from the journey. I have grown from it. I've been made sensitive because of it. And more important than anything else, *I found God in the midst of it.* Maybe even *because of it,* I don't know. It's very possible.

"What have I learned? I've discovered that God is not a crutch for us Christians, Eileen, as some critics choose to argue. I'm quick to respond that crutches are inexpensive and disposable. *God is not.* I've learned that God is more like an iron lung to me now. He's a pacemaker. He's the complete life-support system. He's everything, and I've learned that truth firsthand in my deepest valley. *He is there, and He is sufficient.*

"Do you know what the sweetest times of my life have been? As I looked back yesterday I had to admit many were actually borne right there in my darkest hours. They were the times when I somehow sensed the tug of God's love despite my confusion and fears. Don't ask me how. It was never audible. But quiet. Deep inside. While I cried, perhaps. Or while I read Scripture into the night. Or while I rested, listening and available. And do you know what the worst times of my life have been? This may surprise you like it surprised me: they were the times when I lost sight of God's love. Either failing to believe His individual love for me or forgetting His love for me has sent me into deeper despair than anything I've ever experienced as a child. That's the truth. Even today, if I take my eyes off His love, the bottom drops out.

"You know me well, friend, and you know there are still times of old and new hurts. You know there are past and present limitations that can bring me to a near-halt. That may always bring me to a halt and nag unresolved. Will I ever work through all of this in a lifetime? I wonder. Will I ever know total and complete wholeness here? I don't know. But even if it's not until eternity—not until I'm finally *home*—I pray God sees fit to join the disjointed and let me soar with the eagles. Broken wings and all, I crave air, Eileen. I yearn for flight and wholeness. For my own *A* in Ability.

"For now I'm not too thrilled to be caught up in the struggle of living, and, I admit, progress is often so slow I get discouraged. Life is not easy. It's more meaningful for me now than ever, yet it is not easy. I don't like that fact, but I'm learning to accept it. I find the struggles shift and change as I grow, but they are still there. The truth is, I probably lose more than I win, *but I do win some.*

"I don't think I've ever shared this verse with you before, but it's one of my favorites. It's from James three, and it says, 'For we all stumble in many ways.' I wonder just how many Christians there are who slave so hard to project the image they have everything under control. No problems. No difficulties in their faith or in their personal lives. Do you know what I think? I think they must live in some sort of a mask factory. I think they're hiding, and I think they're discipling scores of others in the church to wear masks too. To me that's tragic. Who or what can break that cycle of deception? I ask you, Eileen, how can we possibly bear one another's burdens in the Kingdom when we're playing games of hide-and-seek? How can we effectively minister to one another's needs in the body of Christ when we don't even know who's really concealed behind the mask? And how can we nourish the hungry sheep in this world when we don't understand what specific food they're starving for? Take it from a veteran actress, masks alienate us from healing and wholeness. They do. They build walls to hold the hurt in and keep the help out. You simply cannot seek to live an authentic Christlike existence on one hand, and hold a mask in the other. The two do not mix.

"Anyway, just like the verse in James says, I stumble and I stumble badly. How freeing it is, though, to be able to say that out loud. *I stumble.* But as my friend I want you to know something this morning: no matter how I fall in one particular area of my life, or flipflop through another and fail miserably, it really is the Father I want to please. It's God I want to serve. It's God I want to share. I want to be His, Eileen, and I want to be a faithful steward of the gifts He's given me. Not just for this special day when I can dedicate *Reaching Out With Love* to His service, but always. That's my deepest dream of all time. *I want to be His.*"

I paused to find Eileen watching me intently. "I'm sorry," I stated apologetically. "I haven't given you a chance to say a thing. Doesn't it bother you when I talk on and on? You've been awfully quiet."

"I don't mind it at all, Jean. Please go on," she encouraged. "I love to listen."

"But I don't mean to talk your ears off."

"You're just too insightful to interrupt today," she shared warmly.

I smiled. "Insightful?" I repeated. "You know something? You've always been the best audience I've ever had. I love you so much. Hey, Eileen—I just got a great idea!" I exclaimed and smacked the table with the palms of my hands for effect. "Want to do lecture tours with me on the road? Huh? You and I could travel from city to city all across America! What do you say? Just think what kind of a team we'd be! We'll plant you in the audience and you can cheer and applaud wildly when I make all those insightful comments you like! Is it a deal? Just imagine your name in lights: EILEEN LOGAN PRESENTS ROOKIE AUTHOR!"

She grinned wide. "Sure, Jean. Sure. I'll do anything to help you out—for about five thousand dollars an engagement."

I could not suppress the hearty laugh that came bursting out. "And all this time I thought it was my charm that held you spellbound! Ha! So much for loyalty and friendship!"

"All right," she said in a compromising tone of voice. "You have spunk, kid. You show promise. I like that. I'm going to give you a special reduction in my rates. How's one thousand dollars a speech sound?"

I faked a chain of coughs and replied, "No way, Eileen. Don't you know you're treading on dangerous ground?"

"Okay," she teased. "You seem to be pretty sharp in business. My final offer is *fifty cents.*"

"YOU'RE HIRED!" I bellowed out and shook her hand enthusiastically. "IT'S A DEAL!"

We both giggled like silly children. It was the cleansing kind of laughter that bridged the years and experiences separating us. When we finally had settled down, Eileen lifted the beverage container from the table, poured a second glass of juice for herself, and asked, "Want more?"

I nodded yes and raised my glass. After we were both refreshed and silent, Eileen noted, "Your bike trip yesterday was certainly productive, to say the least."

"I know," I agreed, "and there's so much more that occurred to me in a newer way. Remember Professor Grimes from college? He wasn't in Bill's department but in Religion and Philosophy. I think he left a couple years ago."

"Of course we remember him. Bill and I had the Grimes family over for supper a couple times. Lovely people."

"Well," I continued, "just about every time I head out on my bike and it's breezy, I think of Dr. Grimes. One time in college he pulled me aside and said, 'Jeanie?' He always called me Jeanie. 'Jeanie?' he said. 'There are two winds in life and we need them both. The first is the wind of adversity. The second is the wind of direction. Through resistance, one forms our character. The other pushes us along on course and keeps our hope alive. God in His wisdom has given us both winds. As a pair united they keep us from growing complacent in one sense, or getting overwhelmed in another. God has richly blessed you with two winds. Never, never curse them, Jeanie. Learn to embrace them both. Together they will make you attain your highest calling, your highest self.'

"Isn't that beautiful? Well, during most of my life my focus has been on the chilling wind of adversity. But there's been another dynamic force involved, the wind of direction. I like to think of that one as the active hand of God. He's given me much to be thankful for, Eileen. Even as a child God blessed me with intelligence and creativity. Then He gave me a host of high school and college activities to cling to when otherwise I would have fallen apart. God led me to a college that did not bombard me with the Truth, but one that gently nudged me to discover Him in non-threatening terms. He gave me a freshman English teacher who made me want to believe. Another teacher who insisted I tell my experiences and write, write, write.

And how can I speak of the encouragement I received from other faculty members who believed in me? I can't. I simply can't.

"Eileen, one of the most precious of all gifts from God's hand has been writing, the art and act of disclosing who I am. I can't believe I'm in my twenties and yet able to see God bring my dreams to pass. Can you? Teaching's been a ministry for me, but writing is what I've always wanted to do. Eileen, I can still recall the very day back in college when I sat teary-eyed in the balcony during a chapel service and felt the tug of God's calling. I breathed, 'Jesus? You give me the gift, You make the way straight, and I will communicate for You all my days. All that I am and all that I have is at Your disposal. Use me, Lord. Use me in writing. Use me in speaking. Use me in Your Kingdom. I'm Yours.' If anything, Eileen, I mean that same prayer more today than ever I did then, and I will be faithful to that promise until I die.

"Something else I remembered yesterday on my bike trip was a poem I wrote. It was the first of my things to be nationally published and it was titled "God, i don't know why you love me, i don't." My first article to be accepted for publication was titled "Love That Makes a Difference." And now my first book, *Reaching Out With Love*. Did you catch the common word in all three? I've spent thousands of hours my whole life thinking about love, what it was and what it wasn't. Today when I think of love I immediately think of God's love and, shortly thereafter, I think of yours. What a beautiful, gentle wind your love has been, Eileen. In a land where everybody finds it easy to talk and sing and preach about love, you stepped out of the crowd and *showed* me.

"Have you ever seen the play *The Miracle Worker?* That's such a terrific story. When I've had the chance to teach it to my classes at school, I've continually been awed by two powerful realities: Helen Keller's savage world of blackness, and Anne Sullivan's persistence to pulse the light inside. Emotionally I was in darkness when you came into my world. Yet, like Anne with Helen, you spelled into the chaos over and over. You told me of my worth, of God's love for me, and of your love for me. I was so blind. You were so patient. Sadly it's taken years, but eventually your words breathed life and light into the barren wasteland. Today I can understand. Today I can receive. Today I can love God back because of you, Eileen. Because you continued to strive with me. You didn't give up.

"In human terms it takes a very special kind of nurse to touch an open cancerous growth and administer healing. That is equally true for emotional and spiritual ills. You are a burden-bearer first class, Eileen. You saw me bruised, wounded, and bleeding, and yet you chose to draw near when it was inconvenient. You actually handled my sores. You cried with me. I could see it in your eyes and I could sense it through your gentle touch: God was loving and reaching me through you. He was teaching me that love doesn't fail.

"If I seem choked up, it's because I am. I can never repay you. I feel so useless trying. I thank God for the dear older sister He's given me in you. You're a friend forever."

Eileen stretched a slender arm across the table and cupped my wrist in her hand. Neither of us spoke. The moment was too cherished to shatter with conversation.

"Anything I have ever given you," Eileen whispered, "you have returned in full. Do you hear me, Jean?"

"But I don't see how," I protested.

"Shh. Just accept it. Don't question it. You have given me so much, Jean, and long before today."

Puzzled, I replied, "If you say so."

"It's true," she confirmed.

"But—"

"It's true. Accept that."

I glanced down to see Eileen's hand still draped over mine. "Eileen? Can I ask you a serious question?"

"Yes, of course."

"It's not something you'll expect," I warned.

"Go ahead," she answered. "Try me."

"It's kind of personal."

"Jean, we've come so far together. What could it be? Just ask."

"All right," I said. "Here goes." I appeared wordless to build the suspense and fought the urge to smile.

"Whatever it is, just ask. I'll do my best to answer," she comforted.

Then the question arrived. *"Eileen? Can I please use your bathroom? I've been dying here for the last half-hour!"*

Our laughter peeled through the house. *"Oh, you!"* I heard Eileen exclaim as I pushed out my chair and flew down the hall. *"Oh, you!"*

When I returned to the kitchen I found Eileen stacking our breakfast dishes at the nearby counter. She was still smiling. "Look at the time," I said.

"I know," she commented and checked the kitchen clock above our heads.

"I have to go and do some last minute things for the dedication gathering. Like I told you earlier, we're expecting a full house. It's so good of my brother Peter and his wife to host this. I'm anxious for you and Bill to meet my family. All of them should be there except Bernie. I'm excited about the party. I know quite a few from my church will be there. Some favorite professors from college. Other friends and fellow teachers.

"I can't wait to see the look on my mother's face when I give her the very first copy of *Reaching Out With Love*. I know she's sacrificed over the years to try to provide what my father lacked, and I want this to be a special day for her. I hope she's proud of me. I hope they're all proud of me. Better late than never.

"And speaking of late, Eileen, I do have to run. Thank you for a wonderful visit together and for breakfast. Next time we'll turn the tables and let you do all the talking, okay?"

"It's a deal," Eileen replied and reached out to hug me.

"Eileen?" I asked.

"What, Jean?"

"I really *do* have a serious question to ask, only this time I'm not kidding."

"Go ahead," she responded. "I'll try my best to answer."

"This is kind of bold, I admit it."

"That's all right, Jean. Ask."

"One of these years if you see that I've grown and matured enough . . . well . . . it might not even be for twenty years, Eileen, maybe even more," I stammered. "Do you think you could ever get me a necklace charm or a special pin . . . and could you maybe have something engraved on it . . . like *A* and *Ability* . . . or something like that? I realize it'll only be a downpayment for the real one later, but I've been thinking how choice that gift would be. You and I will know what it means. And God will know what it means. I won't ask this again, okay? I'll just leave the idea in your hands for your judgment. You know me—I'm always the last person to see my own growth, that's all. It . . . it would just mean a lot."

I turned to go, then looked back into Eileen's face. "How about one more hug for the road?" I said. "I need it today."

She squeezed tightly, and over my shoulder I heard her say, "I love you, Jean Marie."

"I love you too," I said, battling against the lump in my throat. *"You're the best."*

O Lord, how could I end a day like this and not fall on my knees before You in utter gratitude? I felt the waves of love coming from Your people today at the book gathering like I have never felt before. Their faces and words of support and embraces will be etched in my memory forever. Thank You, Father. Thank You for making this launching possible. I am overwhelmed.

As I stood before the crowd of people today I couldn't help but think about the genuine effort it took for everyone to be assembled. We were elbow to elbow. The house overflowing. Although a few people traveled great distances to attend the dedication and others only took twenty or thirty minutes en route, it's taken me all my life to get to that time and place. All my life, Father.

Of any of the presents I've given You (they have not been many), never have I cherished one more than this book. All others combined could not touch the love and eagerness I had in my heart when it came for the official, public time to lay it down for You. You know it was already in Your hands, Father, even before the ideas germinated in my mind. I know that, too. Thank You for giving me this book long enough for me to offer it back. It was sweet and holy to the touch, but it was clearly Yours.

People expect that words are an occupational calling of mine because of what I teach at school and now because of this first book. Words are nice, but I find my skills grossly lacking to express from my heart what I feel for You. I'm not referring to the things You've allowed me to have or the abilities You've allowed me to use, but I'm thinking of my love for You Yourself.

I guess it's a modern day temptation to be preoccupied with our experiences. New songs in the church today stem from our experiences. Books are written of our experiences. Television ministries and sharing groups and sermons pull heavily from personal experiences. Masses of us look to experiences for hope, and we are wrong. We are dead wrong. Thank You for teaching me that hope does not lie in our experiences at all. It lies in You. Only in You. Hope is not in what we do or attempt or sing or write or say or live out. It is exclusively in You. You are our Hope in ages past, You are our Morning Star, You are our Alpha and Omega, not our experiences. Our vision must always be outward, Father, not inward. Our eyes must be fixed upon You as the Author and

Finisher of our faith, not upon one another's experiences, and most certainly not upon our own. Teach me, Lord, and teach Your people to put our hope in You.

It's late and I'm so exhausted right now I hardly know what to say, Lord. Please know my times are in Your hands. I often wonder what You see in me or what You want me for, but I am here bowed before You and I am Yours. Help me. Help me bury the past dead, not alive. Help me consecrate each new day of my life afresh to You. Help me in my tomorrows to press on toward the mark and high calling of Your service. I am Yours, Father. I belong with You.

And there is one last thing tonight, Abba, that must be said. For the wind of adversity, I thank You. For the past hardships along the way that drove me closer to Your side, I thank You. Even for the present aches of unfulfilled desire that remind me today how much I still need you, I thank You. I have learned I would a thousand times rather come afflicted into Your presence, O Great Physician, than be content and healthy apart from You.

So keep me safely abiding in You, Lord. Keep me near and dear to Your heart. Keep me dependent upon Your hand for all that I do. There is no other place I long to be.

You are my Home.

Amen.

Revelation 21:4

. . . and He
shall wipe away
every tear from their eyes;
and there shall no longer be
any death;
there shall no longer be
any mourning,
or crying,
or pain;

the first things
have passed
away.

Amen.